1 CORINTHIANS
2 CORINTHIANS
William Baird

KNOX PREACHING GUIDES
John H. Hayes, Editor

John Knox Press
ATLANTA

Library of Congress Cataloging in Publication Data
Baird, William, 1924-
  1 Corinthians, 2 Corinthians.
  (Knox preaching guides)
  Bibliography: p.
  1. Bible. N.T. Corinthians—Commentaries.
2. Bible. N.T. Corinthians—Homiletical use.
I. Title. II. Series.
BS2675.3.B23   277'.207   79-92064
ISBN 0-8042-3239-3

© copyright John knox Press 1980
10 9 8 7 6 5 4 3 2 1
Printed in the United States of America
John Knox Press
Atlanta, Georgia 30365

Contents

2 CORINTHIANS

Introduction

Paul's letters to the Corinthians may be the most practical books in the NT. They are addressed to specific problems of a particular urban church. Sermonic possibilities are packed into Paul's discussion of basic theological and ethical problems. The preacher should not suppose, however, that problems which Paul addressed find perfect parallels in the modern church. Although the fundamental human problem may be much the same, particular problems have their meaning in their own cultural setting. Paul's ancient instruction must be translated into the idiom of today. At the same time, one should not conclude that Paul's advice on antique issues is without relevance for contemporary ethics. Paul serves as a model for our ethical and theological preaching. In the Corinthian correspondence, he has taken the gospel (the Message of Christ and him crucified) and translated it into terms which are meaningful to people removed in time and space from God's redemptive action in Jesus Christ.

Built beside the azure Gulf of Corinth and nestled beneath the sheer cliff of the Acrocorinth, Corinth was a teeming metropolis in Paul's day. Its location on the narrow isthmus connecting northern and southern Greece had made Corinth a commercial center. Rather than navigate the dangerous passage around the southern cape, many mariners chose to transport their cargo across the isthmus. Corinth was noted for its bronze foundries and an example of its craftmanship can be viewed in the Athens museum—a finely shaped mirror (see 1 Cor 13:12). Crowds surged to the city to attend the Isthmian Games, held biennially, and second only to the Olympian in importance (see 1 Cor 9:24–27). Every kind of religion was represented at Corinth. The city's most impressive architectural ruin is the Temple of Apollo. Corinth was noted for its immorality, though the story about 1,000 sacred prostitutes cavorting atop the Acrocorinth is legendary. Nevertheless, we should not forget that Paul's stern indictment of pagan culture in Rom 1:28–32 was dictated in Corinth.

According to Acts 18, Paul began his work in the Corinthian synagogue, and when driven out, moved to the house of Titius Justus. An inscription which reads "Synagogue of the Hebrews" has been found not far from the triumphal arch which served as entrance to the forum. At Corinth, Paul made the acquaintance of Aquila and Priscilla who shared his trade and came to share his mission. Converts were drawn in the main from the lower classes (1 Cor 1:26), including slaves (1 Cor 7:21), yet the wealthy were also represented. An inscription can be seen near the theater which indicates that the pavement there had been donated by a city official named Erastus—perhaps to be identified with "Erastus, the city treasurer" (Rom 16:23). Toward the end of his eighteen-month stay in the city, Paul was hauled before the newly-appointed governor, Gallio, brother of the Stoic philosopher, Seneca. The traditional place of the hearing, the *bema* or judgment platform, has been discovered in the forum. According to Acts, the governor refused to render judgment on a matter pertaining to religion.

Paul's stormy relationship with the church is chronicled in his letters to the Corinthians. While our NT includes two epistles, some scholars believe Paul wrote as many as eight or nine. For the purpose of this commentary, I will adopt the hypothesis that Paul wrote four letters to Corinth.

(1) Prior to writing 1 Cor, Paul had written an earlier letter to Corinth. Mentioned in 1 Cor 5:9 and dubbed the "previous letter," this epistle has probably been lost.

(2) The second letter is 1 Cor. Although it appears to display disruptions and displacements, 1 Cor can be taken as a single, unified letter. It was written from Ephesus (16:8), probably around A.D. 55.

Before the third letter was written, the relationship between Paul and the church appears to have deteriorated. Hoping to salvage the situation, the apostle made a hurried trip from Ephesus to Corinth and back. This trip, usually depicted as the "painful" or "sorrowful" visit, is reconstructed from statements in 2 Cor.

(3) Since the "painful visit" did not solve the problem, Paul decided to send another letter. Usually characterized as the "severe" or "tearful" letter, this third epistle is described as written "out of much affliction" and "with many tears" (2 Cor 2:4)—a letter which Paul came to regret (2 Cor 7:8). Many scholars believe this letter is to be found in part in 2 Cor 10 – 13.

(4) After sending the severe letter, Paul left Ephesus and traveled to Troas where he had hoped to meet Titus and receive news about the situation in Corinth (2 Cor 2:13). When Titus did not arrive, Paul went on to Macedonia where he met Titus and received his happy report (2 Cor 7:5– 13). A letter was then written to Corinth expressing Paul's joy at the reconciliation which had been accomplished. Although some scholars are convinced that 2 Cor 1– 9, includes fragments from other letters, I believe it is simpler, however, to assume that 2 Cor 1– 9 is a single unit, constituting the bulk of the "reconciliation letter." Nevertheless, the decision to offer simple solutions should not be understood as a suggestion to ignore critical questions. Preaching from any text demands careful attention to its meaning in its historical setting.

1 CORINTHIANS

Address and Thanksgiving
(1 Corinthians 1:1–9)

In writing to his churches Paul follows the form of letters of his day. He is not attempting to write Scripture, but simply to express his message in ordinary fromat. The letter of Paul's day has two conventional features at the beginning: the address and the thanksgiving. The address consists of three parts: (1) the writer introduces himself; (2) the recipients are named; (3) a greeting is expressed.

(1) Paul introduces himself as "an apostle of Christ Jesus." The term "apostle" is a transliteration of a Greek word which depicts a person sent with a commission, representing an important authority—someone like an ambassador (see 2 Cor 5:20). Paul is reflecting his conversion experience when he preceived that God "had set me apart before I was born and had called me through his grace" (Gal 1:15). Like Jeremiah (Jer 1:5), Paul had been destined for apostleship before he could act on his own. God always has priority in the call to prophetic ministry, and this is especially true for Paul who considered himself "least of the apostles, unfit to be called an apostle" (15:9). Joined with Paul is Sosthenes, a companion, but not co-author, who is known to the Corinthians. He may be the Sosthenes of Acts 18:17.

(2) The letter is addressed to the church at Corinth. Here Paul used te term *ekklesia*—a word which finds its background

in the OT idea of the assembly of God's people. The preacher needs to remember that the church is primarily people, not architectural edifice or institutional structure. I can imagine Paul as he writes envisaging the people of God, assembled to observe the Lord's Supper in a Corinthian house, listening to the reading by lamplight of a letter from an apostle. About these people, Paul says two astonishing things: "they are sanctified in Christ Jesus"; they are "called saints." The words "sanctified" and "saints" come from the same root and describe a holy people, set apart by the call of God. In view of what he has heard from Chloe's people (1:11), it appears to us preposterous that Paul could call the Corinthians saints; their halos were tarnished at best. Yet, this reminds us of an important truth and useful homiletical theme: holiness is not a human achievement, but a response to God's call (see Rom 8:30). Though they look like a tiny island in a sea of paganism, the Christians at Corinth are part of a larger land. They belong with "all those everywhere who call on the name of our Lord Jesus Christ" (v. 2; NIV). The church in Corinth (or in our home town) is but a local expression of the larger, universal body of Christ (see 12:27).

(3) In expressing the greeting, Paul combines Greek and Hebrew expressions: grace (*charis*) and peace (*shalom*). Grace is the gift of God through Christ (2 Cor 8:9), and peace (something sorely needed in Corinth) results from the new relationship which God's gift has made possible (Rom 5:1).

The second main feature of the letter-beginning is the conventional thanksgiving. Although Paul is thankful for the Corinthians, the basis of his thanksgiving is what God has done in them: the grace of God, given in Christ. Grace is God's free gift of righteousness, grounded in his love, and revealed in Christ (Rom 3:24). As v. 6 indicates, this gift of righteousness is disclosed in the "testimony of Christ," that is, in the basic preaching of the Christian gospel. Although materially poor, the Corinthians have been made rich by the gifts of Christ (see 2 Cor 8:9). Among these riches are gifts of speech (or word) and knowledge. The former may include speaking in tongues, but Paul probably intends to stress the more important word of the apostle, prophet, and teacher (12:28). The gift of knowledge (a special problem at Corinth) is not the knowledge which puffs up (8:1), but the wisdom of God revealed in the

crucified Christ (1:24). Above all, these temporary gifts (13:8 –
9) should be seen in the context of the ultimate—the fulfil-
ment of the final purposes of God. The time of triumph will also be the time of judgment—the OT day of the Lord (Amos
5:18). The Christians, however, can face this final test without
fear, for they can count on the faithfulness of God, already experienced in the "fellowship of his son."

Although this text is packed with many sermonic possibilities—the "faithfulness of God," "life in view of the ultimate"—I believe I would put major emphasis on the idea of
the church. Here a variety of motifs might be developed: the
church in the city or in the midst of pagan culture; the church
as people of God; the church local and universal; Christians as
saints and sinners; Christians as poor and rich; gospel, grace
and gifts.

The Danger of Disunity
(1 Corinthians 1:10–4:21)

Factions in Corinth (1:10– 17)

After completing the conventional introduction, Paul considers the problem of factionalism. Taking up a style which he uses for ethical appeals (see Rom 12:1), the apostle exhorts the Corinthians to agree with one another (literally, "say the same thing") and to avoid divisions. The term for division can describe a tear which results from sewing a new patch on an old garment (Mark 2:21). Paul also urges the Corinthians to be "united in the same mind and the same judgment." The word "united" is used in Mark 1:19 to depict the mending of nets. Paul's advice to say and think the same thing should not be taken as a demand for uniformity. Later in the letter, Paul shows that his own "opinion" (the word used here for "judgment") is held with flexibility (7:25). Unity, not uniformity, is required. Moreover, unity is not to be attained by institutional manipulation, but by sound mind and judgment.

The character of Corinth's disunity has been reported by Chloe's people. Chloe is probably a resident of Corinth. Her people may be members of her household who have visited Paul in Ephesus. According to their report, there is quarreling among the Corinthian Christians. The word for quarreling is listed as one of the vices of the pagans in Rom 1:29, and included among the works of the flesh in Gal 5:20. In Corinth, this strife is expressed in party slogans: "I belong to Paul," etc. When Paul observes that "Each one of you says," he stresses the heedless individuality of the slogans—an emphasis confirmed by the use of the emphatic first person pronoun. The implication is: *"I* belong to Paul, and you don't!" "I belong to Paul, and I'm proud of it!"

All sorts of attempts have been made to identify the Corinthian factions. Some have supposed that there is really only one faction—that Paul aims his arguments in 1 Cor at a single group. Yet, given the variety of converts within a pluralistic society, a minister in Corinth (or any other church, for that matter) would be considered fortunate to be faced with only one set of opponents. When efforts at identification are made, the party of Paul is usually supposed to consist of "charter members"—converts of Paul who remain loyal to their original leader. The Apollos group, according to this approach, would be identified as devotees of the eloquent Alexandrian preacher who worked for a time in Corinth (Acts 18:24– 19:1). Some interpreters have supposed that Paul's criticism of eloquence (1:17; 2:1) is directed at Apollos and his friends, but the apostle's clear support of his ministerial colleague (4:6) refutes this supposition. Cephas ("rock") no doubt is to be identified as Simon Peter, for Paul often refers to him by this Aramaic version of his nickname (9:5; Gal 2:11). The reference here has encouraged speculation about an actual ministry in Corinth on Peter's part—a ministry which might have resulted in a party of Christians distinctly loyal to the Jerusalem leaders.

Most problematic is the Christ-party. Some think this slogan is Paul's: "You may belong to Paul or Apollos, but as for me, I belong to Christ." By way of contrast, other scholars believe the Christ-party constitutes the locus of the major opposition to Paul (see 2 Cor 10:7). I believe all we can say for sure is that factions existed within the Corinthian church. It would be a mistake, too, to imagine that the Corinthian factions represent close parallels to modern denominations. The Corinthians had not divided into separated communities, for one letter could be addressed to all. This, of course, does not mean that our text is without significance for the proclamation of Christian unity. Factions can (and do) become divisions, and Paul's analysis of the cause (e.g. inordinate loyalty to leaders) and the cure (the word of the cross) provides abundant resources for preaching.

Paul begins his refutation of factionalism by raising three questions. The first of these implies that Christ cannot be divided—that factions are a denial of the nature of the church as the one body of Christ (12:12–13). The other two questions are expressed in a Greek construction which implies a negative answer: "Paul was not crucified for you, was he?" (NASB). Paul attacks the group which boasts loyalty to himself, and shows the theological impossibility of their position. Christ, not Paul was crucified for them, and they were "baptized into Christ" (Gal 3:27), not in the name of Paul. In pagan cults, devotees were prone to maintain loyalty to the priest who performed the rites of their initiation. Paul insists that this is impossible in his case, since he baptized so few—maybe enough for a committee, not a faction! Although he remembered Crispus, once ruler of a synagogue (Acts 18:8), and Gaius, later his host in Corinth (Rom 16:23), Paul almost blundered into forgetting the household of Stephanas, his "first converts in Achaia" (16:15). The possibility that Paul may have forgotten others comes as a shock to modern preachers preoccupied with ministerial records and evangelistic statistics.

Although baptism is not unimportant (see 12:13), Christ had not sent Paul to baptize but to preach the gospel—the primary responsibility of every preacher. In his mission, Paul does not stress baptizing, which can divide, but preaching the gospel of the crucified Christ, which condemns factionalism and lays bare the ground for unity. The word for preaching is used in Paul's world for the announcement of important events—the birth of a prince, victory in battle. In those days, news traveled slowly. Word of victory in a distant battle, for example, could not be received until the herald arrived. During the time of his coming, those awaiting news continued in war-time anxiety. Only after the message actually arrived did victory become a reality. Thus, the announcement itself became an event which made the original happening available to the hearer. This is why Paul describes the good news as an act—"the power of God to salvation" (Rom 1:16). In proclaiming the event, distracting rhetoric should be avoided. A sermon which dazzles the hearer with fancy homiletical footwork can nullify the cross. I believe the converse is also implied: the way the cross of Christ becomes a powerful event is through the preaching of the gospel. This text depicts the awesome power and grave responsibility of those of us who dare to mount the pulpit stairs.

The Word of the Cross (1:18–2:5)

The gospel which Paul had been sent to preach is "the word of the Cross"—a word which stands in judgment on the factionalism of Corinth. To describe this word, Paul speaks paradoxically: The word is folly ("complete absurdity," NAB) to some and the power of God to others. For those who are perishing—that is, those who reject the gospel and stand under its judgment (Rom 1:18)—it is foolishness. For those who are being saved—that is, those who are called (v. 24) and respond in faith (v. 21)—it is the power of God. Though "perishing" and "being saved" depict the final outcome of human life (see 15:18; 5:5), the processes have already begun. The word, like the preaching of the OT prophets, is a dynamic event. God works in it for judgment or salvation (Rom 1:16).

To develop his argument, Paul quotes the Greek translation of Isa 29:14. According to this version, God intends to destroy the "wisdom of the wise." Paul's exegesis, which takes the form of three questions, asserts that God's intention has been accomplished. One can ask, "Where is the wise man?" The fact that no one with genuine wisdom can be found proves that God has made foolish the wisdom of the world. Paul's list of three professional pundits shows his effort to be universal: the "wise man" is the Greek sophist; the "scribe" is the Jewish teacher; the "debator" (or "researcher") is like the Athenians, looking for something new (Acts 17:21).

Paul, of course, does not deny that the sophists and scribes know something; he's been to graduate school, too! What he affirms is that "the world did not know *God* through Wisdom." The intellectuals know things; they do not know God! A sermon on the knowledge of God or the doctrine of revelation could be developed from this text. In God's wisdom, that is, according to God's way of revelation, God remains hidden from human scrutiny; by his very nature, God is not an object which the human mind can comprehend. Instead, God discloses his will in a shocking manner: he decided to save people by the foolishness of preaching.

The word for preaching is *kerygma*, that is, the message of the herald. Basically, it means "proclamation," and can be used for either the act of proclaiming or the content of the message. Paul's stress on the "folly" of preaching does not mean that preaching is intrinsically foolish, or that preaching (like some heard on the radio) should strive for a new level of absurdity. The proclamation is foolish because of its content—the crucified Christ. Every preacher needs to be reminded, too, that what God accomplishes through preaching is not intellectual enlightment, but human salvation. To believe does not mean primarily to assent to the doctrine of the *kerygma*, but to entrust one's life to the Christ of the cross.

The call to faith is an affront to human expectation. The "Jews demand signs" ("miracles" JB), that is, they want supernatural proof that faith is worth the risk. The "Greeks seek wisdom," that is, they want philosophical argument or mystical omen that the message merits belief. "Jews" and "Greeks" represent the universal quest for easy security rather than costly commitment. They epitomize a persistent pride which demands that God's revelation conform to human standards—a pride which ought to be addressed by our preaching. By way of contrast, the apostles proclaim the crucified messiah. Although this message meets a special need in Corinth, Paul everywhere stresses the centrality of the cross (see Gal 3:1). When he says that Christ crucified is a "stumblingblock," Paul may be speaking autobiographically. The message of the early Christians—that a man executed by the Romans was the messiah—appeared to be blasphemy to Paul. For him to accept the crucified one as messiah demanded a radical reinterpretation of God's way of working—that God achieved his purposes not through might, but through weakness, that the messiah was not powerful king, but suffering servant (an appropriate theme for a sermon).

Yet, "to those who are called, both Jews and Greeks" (the call is universal), the crucified Christ is the power and wisdom of God. Again, the crucified one is power and wisdom only to those who respond to God's call in faith (1:18). To these, the concepts of power and wisdom have been completely revised. The scandal of the gospel is that God's "power is made perfect in weakness" (2 Cor 12:9): the ultimate power behind the universe is God's suffering love. The foolishness of the gospel is that God's wisdom is disclosed in Jesus Christ: the ultimate meaning of reality is incarnate in him. In an age of atomic power and electronic calculators, this message is a stumbling block to scientists and foolishness to philosophers. Paul's point is summarized paradoxically:

　　the foolishness of God is wiser . . .
　　the weakness of God is stronger . . .

Having shown that the word of the cross stands in judgment on Corinthian factionalism, Paul proceeds to argue that the Corinthians have no ground for pride. He urges them to consider the circumstances in which they received the Christian message. Not many of them were wise, powerful or noble. The first term has been used in v. 20 to depict the professional intellectuals, and the second and third describe persons of political and social rank. Paul's evaluation of the congregation indicates that most of the Corinthian Christians were from the lower classes. In this situation God acted in an astounding way: he chose the lowly and shamed the mighty. That God's election (see Rom 8:33) is according to grace is seen in the object of his choice—the foolish, the weak, the ignoble, that is, the opposites of the three classes listed in the preceding verses. God's positive action has a negative effect: he shamed the wise and the strong; he brought to naught those who imagine they are something. A sermon could be developed on the theme, "the Scandal of Grace."

As a result of God's action no human can boast. If they are nothing on their own, and if they are what they are by God's grace, what can the Corinthians boast about? Indeed, the attempt to boast in the presence of God is the nadir of human sinfulness. The new situation of believers is the result of God's action in Christ "whom God made our wisdom" (see 1:24). As we have seen (v. 21) wisdom is not an intellectual but a soteriological term. Thus, Paul characterizes the wisdom which is revealed in Christ as righteousness, sanctification, and redemption. "Righteousness" depicts the basic relation to God made possible by his grace received in faith (Rom 3:21–26). "Sanctification" (or consecration) represents a style of life set apart for holiness and empowered by God's spirit (6:11). "Redemption" is God's action whereby freedom from slavery is purchased and adoption to sonship is attained (Gal 4:4–5). The three terms could provide an outline for a sermon summarizing the whole of Christian experience. The conclusions from Scripture (Jer 9:24) makes Paul's point crystal clear: if one wants to boast, one must boast (or glory) in God.

Just as they have no basis for pride in themselves, so the Corinthians can find no ground for boasting in their ministers. Paul makes this case by describing his own conduct at Corinth. He came to proclaim the "testimony of God," to preach the gospel. In carrying out this purpose, Paul avoided fancy rhetoric (see 1:17). He decided to know nothing except "Christ and him crucified." To know nothing but Christ, does not mean to reduce theological knowledge to its barest minimum. If that were the case, Paul should never have written the rest of this letter, let alone the Epistle to the Romans. As a thoughtful sermon could point out, to know nothing but Christ is to know everything significant. Christ is the key unlocking the depths of divine wisdom (see 2:6– 16).

In conducting his ministry Paul was with the Corinthians "in weakness and much fear and trembling" (v. 3). The latter two terms represent an OT concept which Paul uses elsewhere to express awe in the presence of God's action (Phil 2:12). Paul was not afraid of physical danger (see 2 Cor 11:24– 29). Instead, his fear acknowledges the frailty of humans who purport to speak for God—a fear which every preacher ought to emulate. In delivering that proclamation, Paul's speech (word) and his message *(kerygma)* "were not with wise and persuasive words" (v. 4; NIV). Rather, he adopted a style which allowed the spirit (the reality and power of God's presence) to function (see 1 Thess 1:5). It was a good thing he did, too, for otherwise people might have had faith in the rhetorical skill of Paul. As it was, their faith was grounded in the power of God.

It is sometimes supposed that Paul is opposed to homiletics. This view fails to note that Paul uses effective rhetoric throughout his epistles. He is opposed to a contrived and artificial style of preaching which calls attention to itself. To preach Christ so that people can hear, demands careful preparation and effective delivery. The lesson to be learned from Paul is that the form of preaching must conform to the content of the message. A sermon which does not preach Christ— which does not reflect contemporary problems in the judging and redeeming light of the cross—is no sermon at all! It is also supposed that Paul has changed his tactics at Corinth. After an unsuccessful mission at Athens, Paul abandoned philosophical speculation and began to preach Christ crucified. I find such exegesis unconvincing. To know nothing but Christ and him crucified had been Paul's method all along.

The Wisdom of God and the Mind of Christ
(2:6– 3:4)

Though not many Christians were wise, and though their ministers did not preach with "persuasive words of wisdom," Paul asserts that he is able to impart a kind of wisdom. Does this mean that Paul, beyond the basic message of the crucified Christ, intends to dispense an advanced form of doctrine to an elite within the church? In support of an affirmative answer, Paul says that he speaks this wisdom to the "mature," or, as he later calls them, the "spiritual" (vv. 13,15)—terms which describe the initiates or superior members of the Greco-Roman cults. Moreover, Paul claims that he communicates this wisdom "in a mystery" and that it is a "hidden" wisdom which comprehends the "depths of God" (v. 10)—terms which represent the "secret" and mysterious knowledge disclosed to the inner circles of hellenistic religion. Most convincing, Paul says that he fed the Corinthians "with milk, not solid food" (3:2), implying that he dispenses two kinds of doctrine—one elementary, one advanced.

In spite of this evidence, I believe Paul does not intend to suggest that he communicates an esoteric wisdom. He is arguing against a Corinthian factionalism fostered by a proud wisdom which supposes that some Christians are better than others. For him to affirm a ministry of special wisdom to special people would be devastating to his argument. Bcsides, Paul is describing a wisdom which has been revealed in history. It is not a wisdom of the present evil age which is under the dominion of demonic forces (see 2 Cor 4:4; Rom 8:38)—the "rulers of this age" whose power is doomed to destruction. It is the wisdom which these rulers did not understand—the wisdom of God revealed in the Lord of glory whom they crucified. In other words, the wisdom discussed here is integrally related to the crucified Christ, the wisdom and power of God (1:24). Apparently, Paul is not depicting an esoteric wisdom, but the deeper implications of Christ as wisdom of God—the wisdom "which God decreed before the ages for our glorification." The hidden wisdom of God encompasses the whole drama of redemption, and the meaning of this drama is disclosed in Jesus Christ.

If my interpretation is correct, what are we to make of

Paul's distinction between milk and solid food? Probably the distinction implies that the profound message of Christ is reduced to simplicity by the way in which it is received. Just as the gospel is folly to some and power to others (1:18), so Paul's message is milk to some (the babes in Christ) and meat to others (the mature).

Those who have accepted the crucified one as Lord have received God's revelation through the spirit. What they have received can be described as "the hidden depths of God's purposes" (v. 10; TEV). That the Scripture spoke of such things is indicated by Paul's phrase, "it is written." Yet, the quotation appears to be a composite of texts like Isa 52:15; 64:4; Jer 3:16, probably quoted from memory. At any rate, these hidden intentions of God have been revealed by the spirit. To show how the spirit functions in revelation, Paul adopts an analogy. He says that no one can know the things ("thoughts") of a person, that is, a person's intent and inner purposes, except the spirit or mind of that person. In the same way, no one can comprehend the things of God except the spirit of God. The application is clear: since the apostles (and the mature believers) have received "the spirit from God," they can understand his purposes and appreciate his gifts. In 12:28, Paul indicates that the higher gifts can involve the appointment of apostles and teachers—those who have been given the word of wisdom and the word of knowledge (12:8). On the basis of these gifts, Paul is able to speak in words "taught by the Spirit, interpreting spiritual truths to those who possess the Spirit" (v. 13).

By way of contrast, the "unspiritual" or natural person does not receive or understand the gifts of the spirit. Such people are later described as "ordinary men" (3:3) or "merely men" (3:4). The spiritual person, on the other hand, can understand or evaluate all things, even the depths of God. That person cannot be judged, that is, cannot (like the spirit of man, v. 11) become the mere object of human evaluation. Only God (not Paul's critics in Corinth) is the proper judge (4:3–4). Support for Paul's line of argument is drawn from Isa 40:13 (see Rom 11:34). However, when the OT asked, "Who can know the mind of the Lord?" (Hebrew: "spirit of Yahweh"), the obvious answer was "Nobody!" Paul's exegesis is astounding: "We have the mind of Christ." The believer

who has received the spirit understands the redemptive purposes of God; the hidden wisdom of God has been disclosed in
Jesus Christ.

Paul applies this understanding of wisdom to the situation in Corinth. He says that he could not address the Corinthians as spiritual persons, but as people "of the flesh." The
Corinthians are not simply unspiritual persons, they actually
live under the power of sin. The indictment is qualified, however, when Paul depicts his hearers as "babes in Christ." Since
they are "in Christ," the Corinthians cannot be totally devoid
of the spirit (12:13). Like all believers they have received this
gift (1:7), but they have not allowed the spirit to lead them to
maturity. Proof of their spiritual immaturity is seen in the
persistence of "jealously and strife" in their midst—behavior
which can be identified as "works of the flesh" (Gal 5:20). The
charge that the Corinthians behave like ordinary people is
confirmed by their party slogans, "I belong to Paul," etc. The
presence or absence of the spirit is evidenced in ethical
behavior.

The complexity of this text should not discourage homiletical use. An inexhaustible theme is sounded by "the depths
of God"—the whole drama of redemption which unfolds its final act in the crucifixion of Christ. The possessing of "the
mind of Christ" could be treated paradoxically: the arrogance
of its claim and the humiliation of its content (the cross). The
importance of "Christian maturity" is obvious, though the
dullness of the theme might be brightened by the topic,
"Childlike Faith and Childish Behavior" (with a cross-
reference to Mark 10:15). An interesting sermon might be developed on the phrase "ordinary men" (getting rid of the sex-
ist language, of course). In a time when we are called upon to
celebrate our humanity (and rightly so), something more may
be expected of Christians: not to be ordinary persons, but to
be distinctive in our humanity—to celebrate the possibility of
the new humanity which God provides.

Ministers as Servants and Builders (3:5–23)

Having observed that the Corinthian slogans betray immaturity, Paul asks, What, after all, are Apollos and Paul?
They are "servants" —a term which later was used for "dea-
cons"—but in Paul's time stood for ordinary household ser-

vants, table-waiters. The purpose of this servants ministry is to win persons to faith, and ministers are appointed to their tasks by the Lord (God). To show that the success of this ministry depends on God's initiative, Paul borrows an analogy from agriculture. "I planted," that is, Paul was the founder of the faith in Corinth (v. 10; 4:15). "Apollos watered," that is, a later ministry was carried on by the preacher from Alexandria (Acts 18:24– 19:1). Through these various ministries, "God made things grow" (JB). As any farmer knows, what he does in planting and irrigation is mere facilitating the growth which the Creator gives. V. 7 can be translated in a way which is homiletically useful: "So neither he who plants nor he who waters is anything, but God who gives the growth is everything."

As facilitators of God's action, the ministers have work to perform. In this labor they are "equal" (literally, "one"), yet each will receive a wage in accord with effectiveness of service (see v. 14). Since the servants are one in ministry, they are "partners working together for God" (v. 9; TEV). Actually, the text can be translated, "God's fellow-workers"—a description used for Timothy in 1 Thess 3:2 (see 2 Cor 6:1).

Paul concludes the discussion saying, "you are God's field" (i.e. you, the community of faith, are the locus of God's activity); but then, he abruptly changes the metaphor: "You are God's building." The description of the church by either the agricultural or the architectural metaphor offers possibilities for preaching. Apparently, Paul believes other features of the ministry can be reflected by depicting the minister as "master builder." Paul's ministry of building is "according to the grace of God" (v. 10; NASB; see Gal 1:15), and the metaphor of building stresses the importance of the foundation. When Paul says, "I laid a foundation," he is describing his pioneer ministry in Corinth (2:1– 5; Acts 18:1– 18). Though Paul does not like to "build on another man's foundation" (Rom 15:20), that is what other ministers (e.g. Apollos) have done at Corinth. The character of the foundation demands care in building. Indeed, the one and only foundation, Jesus Christ, is the criterion by which all our ministerial activity is measured (2:2). Some have supposed that Paul is taking a back-hand slap at a view of the ministry of Cephas which later appeared in the synoptic tradition (Matt 16:18), but this seems unlikely.

I don't think Paul is discussing different foundations here, but
varying qualities of building.

To differentiate qualities of service, Paul lists various
building materials in descending order. Yet, whereas we
would expect him to mention granite or marble, Paul begins
with gold and silver, and ends with hay and straw. There seem
to be two reasons for this strange development of the metaphor: (1) Paul wants to illustrate varying quality of work; (2)
he wants to emphasize durability of the building. In connection with the latter point, Paul envisages the time of testing:
"the day," that is, the eschatological judgment. The work of
ministry—its faithfulness to the gospel, its effectiveness for
eliciting faith and building community (1 Thess 5:11)—faces
an ultimate test. The supreme test for a building in a hellenistic city was fire. In the same way, the test of our ministry is the
durability of its work—does the community which it builds
survive or "burn up." If the work survives, that is, if the
church continues "to stand fast in the Lord" (1 Thess 2:8), the
minister will receive a reward or wage (v. 8). This reward,
however, seems to be nothing more than successful work itself, "For you are our glory and joy (1 Thess 2:20; see 1 Cor
9:18). In spite of inadequate work, the minister will be
saved—barely ("through fire"). The message to be preached
is: salvation is by grace; ministry demands responsible work.

The metaphor of the church as building suggests a related
figure: the community as temple of God (v. 16). In the Greco-
Roman world, temples were not places to assemble for worship, but houses for the gods. "You" (plural), the church, can
be the dwelling of God, because the spirit of God resides in the
community of faith. The attempt to destroy the temple will result in the destruction of the destroyer. This respect for the
church assumes a basic religious idea: the temple as house of
God is made holy by his presence. The church, even composed
of Corinthian (and modern) sinners (6:9–11), is holy—set
apart to embody God's presence. The statement, "that temple
you are" (v. 17) is a homiletical text which affirms the Pauline
indicative: You are holy, it also implies the Pauline imperative: Become what you are.

Finally, Paul warns that people should not deceive themselves by supposing they are wise. To imagine that one is wise
"in this age" (v. 18) is to embrace the proud wisdom of the

world (1:20; see 8:1). By way of contrast, Paul writes a strange prescription for wisdom which could become a provocative text for a sermon: "become a fool" in order to "become wise." He is not advocating intellectual suicide, but promoting the risk of faith, calling his hearers to identify with the cross so as to receive the true wisdom of God (1:24). To prove that the pretentious wisdom of the world is folly with God (see 1:20), Paul quotes from Job 5:13 and Ps 94:11.

Paul's concluding statement, expressed with rhetorical skill, presents a paradoxical criticism of Corinthian boasting. Though their pride in Paul and Apollos claims too much, the Apostle asserts that they appropriate too little. Actually, "all things are yours" (v. 21), and you should not confess exclusive loyalty to Paul, Apollos, or Cephas, but claim the riches of all. Similarly, in our time, one segment of Christendom should not cling tightly to its exclusive tradition, but enjoy the treasures of the entire Christian heritage. Yet, beyond this, Paul says that "the world or life or death or the present or the future" are yours—a text for a sermon on the theme: "Heirs of God." Here Paul appears to affirm the eschatological idea that the faithful people of God are the heirs of his riches who will share in his reign (see 2 Cor 6:10). Yet, though they are "heirs of God" (Rom 8:17), Christians must make this claim with radical humility. For though all things belong to them, they belong to Christ. To be "fellow heirs" with him (Rom 8:17) means to "share his sufferings" (Phil 3:10) and acknowledge his lordship (Phil 2:11). Yet, beyond this revelation in Christ stands the transcendent God in his hiddenness (Rom 1:20) whose ways are not our ways (Isa 55:8).

Stewards of the Mysteries of God (4:1–21)

After the exalted poetry of the preceding paragraph, Paul returns to the questions of 3:5. His answers provide texts which will prove especially useful in addressing leaders of the church. The ministers, Paul says, should be viewed as "servants of Christ" and "stewards of the mysteries of God." The word for "servant" here is not the same as that used in 3:15. The term used here can describe the "under-rower"—the enslaved oarsman in the lowest deck of a Greek ship. However, it can also be used for various kinds of assistants, e.g. the individual who carries the weapons of a warrior. The steward, on the other hand, is an overseer or manager. According to Paul, he is the administrator of the "mysteries of God." The mysteries have to do with the saving purposes of God revealed in Jesus Christ (2:7; Rom 11:25). The basic requirement of stewards is that they be "found trustworthy." That is, they must carry out the orders of their master faithfully. As ultimately responsible to the Lord, ministers should not be judged by human agencies. Paul does not even judge himself, though that does not mean he is above criticism. Judgment should not be pronounced before the final judgment—the judgment which occurs at the coming of the Lord (Rom 2:16). Though one might expect that the disclosure of hidden things and the secrets of men's hearts would mean condemnation, Paul emphasizes the commendation which the minister will receive from God. This suggests that Paul expects his ministry to be affirmed. In our ministry, too, human evaluation counts for little; both judgment and commendation come from God.

In applying this to himself and Apollos, Paul finds neither Corinthian pride in their preachers nor Corinthian criticism of their ministers to be appropriate. Indeed, Paul warns the Corinthians "not to exceed what is written" (v. 6; NASB). Paul is apparently advising his hearers "to live according to Scripture"—an appropriate homiletical theme. They should adopt a life-style characterized by obedience to God—a style of life which Corinthian factionalism betrays. Again it is evident that pride is the root of the problem. The Corinthians are "puffed up" (an expression used six times in 1 Cor), inflated with a divisive egocentrism. To counter their boasting, Paul says "Who sees anything special in you" (v. 7; Goodspeed). As he has already observed, the Corinthians are nothing on their own; what they are is the result of God's grace. Since all they have is God's gift, the possibility of boasting is obliterated.

Paul develops his criticism of Corinthian pride in an impressive rhetorical expression, heavily punctuated with sarcasm (vv. 8–13). Apparently, the Corinthians imagined that the benefits of the coming kingdom were theirs already. They suppose that they are already "filled" (satiated with the abundance of promised blessings), "rich" (heirs of the expected rewards), and living already like royalty. In sarcastic response, Paul says, "How I wish that you really had become kings so that we might be kings with you!" (v. 8; NIV). If the Corinthians were correct, the apostles, too, would be enjoying the promised blessings of the new age. Proof that the kingdom has not yet come, however, is seen in the plight of the apostles. This plight is described in metaphors borrowed from the Roman arena—metaphors which provide vivid illustrations for a sermon on the ministry. Paul says that the apostles have become a "spectacle" to everybody, even to the angels who rule the cosmic order. The word "spectacle" is the Greek term for "theater." As exhibited "last of all" (v. 9), the ministers are like the final act in the coliseum—gladiators destined to die. In contrast to the Corinthians who suppose themselves to be wise, strong, and honorable, the apostles are fools for Christ (3:18) whose weakness and dishonor points to the power of God (2 Cor 12:9-10). Further evidence that the kingdom has not already arrived is seen in apostolic hardships. The apostles suffer physical deprivations (2 Cor 11:24-29) and support their ministry with manual labor (1 Thess 2:9). Yet, in all of this—reviled, persecuted, slandered—they are examples of the meaning of Christian non-retaliation (Matt 5:38-42). Paul concludes the paragraph with a final figure: the ministers have become like refuse or offscouring, the garbage of the world.

At v. 14, Paul changes his tone; sarcasm gives way to pastoral care. As a father (1 Thess 2:11), Paul admonishes the Corinthians like "beloved children." A father, in contrast to a guide or tutor, admonishes rather than shames. Paul has become their spiritual father by instigating their birth to the Christian faith. Of course, the agent of their conversion was Christ and the means was the gospel. Paul's reference to tutors (RSV: "guides") could be misleading, since the Greek tutor or pedagogue did not provide instruction, but conducted the pupil to school and participated in his discipline. Since he is their father, Paul can urge the Corinthians to "be imitatiors of me." The Corinthians (and our parishioners) should be encouraged to pattern their lives according to the apostolic model—a model consistent with Christ's humility. "Be imitators of me, as I am of Christ" (11:1).

Timothy has been sent to Corinth—as example of what a "beloved and faithful child" ought to be. He, too, had been converted under Paul's guidance (Acts 16: 1) and was worthy to be described as "God's fellow-worker" (1 Thess 3:2; NASB).

He will remind the Corinthians of the "ways" which Paul teaches in every church. The term "way" is frequently used in early Christian literature to describe the ethical life, and for Paul, the more excellent way is love (12:31). Though Timothy has been sent, Paul plans to visit Corinth himself. When the apostle is present, he will find out if the charges of his opponents consist of substance or mere talk. The kingdom of God is not a matter of empty words, but the powerful action of God. Though the kingdom has not yet come, God's power is already at work, judging the pretensions of people. As a father, Paul makes his final plea, "Shall I come with stern discipline (with a rod) or with love in a spirit of gentleness" (see Gal 6:1).

Looking back over chap. 4, I see major themes which deserve homiletical development. Basic is the paradoxical understanding of the ministry to which God's faithful are called. The minister is both lowly servant and overseeing manager; the minister is slandered by people, but commended by God; the minister is loving parent and stern disciplinarian. All of this is depicted in colorful imagery drawn from daily life—the economy and the family, the theater and the garbage heap. Also significant is the theme of eschatology—a topic which, in face of the current uproar about the end of the world, needs to be addressed. Though the end has not yet come, it surely will, bringing its ultimate evaluation of life and ministry. Though the kingdom has not yet arrived, and though Christians do not "have it made," the triumph of the future is sure. God's rule which is coming is present in power to judge and redeem.

The Threat of Immorality
(1 Corinthians 5:1 – 6:20)

Incest and Excommunication (5:1– 13)

Paul turns to a new topic: sexual morality. The frankness with which Paul addresses this important issue can become an example for the modern church. The kind of immorality practiced at Corinth is serious. Not even pagans, whose sexual laxity is a frequent target of Jewish censure, are guilty of this: a member of the congregation is having sexual relations with his father's wife. The way Paul describes the situation suggests that the woman is the violator's step-mother. She may be divorced from the father, or he may be dead; no reference is made to adultery. In any case, the practice is a violation of both Roman and Jewish law (Lev 18:7– 8). Paul is concerned not only with the individual, but especially with the church. Shocked by their attitude, he exclaims, "And you can still be proud of yourselves!" (NEB). Paul does not mean that they are proud because of their immorality, but in spite of it. Boasting (v. 6) and arrogance (4:6, 8) characterize the style of Corinthian religiosity. Rather than arrogance, their attitude should be marked by mourning, and penitent sorrow should move the Corinthians to action: the guilty person ought to be removed from the congregation.

Although Paul has already reached this decision, he believes the church should concur. Though not present, Paul is with the Corinthians in spirit. It is not entirely clear how the phrases "the name of the Lord Jesus" and "the power of the Lord Jesus" fit into the sentence structure, but Paul no doubt uses these expressions to insist that the decision is to be made with sensitivity to the potent presence of the Lord.

The interpretation of v. 5 bristles with difficulties. "Deliver this man to Satan" is another way to recommend excommunication; put him out of the church and into the world where Satan rules (2 Cor 4:4). The "day of the Lord" refers to the final judgment (Rom 2:5). "His spirit" probably means the person's inner self which is somehow to be saved. The "destruction of the flesh" could mean physical death, but it seems unlikely that Paul would advocate salvation by death. Moreover, the idea that the spirit is to be saved when the body is destroyed smacks of hellenistic dualism or notions about the indelibility of baptism. More likely, Paul is implying that the serious condemnation which excommunication entails will provoke a genuine repentance which can lead finally to salvation.

To support his point, Paul draws an analogy from the Passover. Just as a diligent search must be made to eradicate leaven from the Jewish household, so an earnest effort must be made to put immorality out of the congregation. This is necessary because "a little yeast works through the whole batch of dough" (v. 6; NIV). Although Paul implies that sin is contagious, his main emphasis is that one case of corruption contaminates the whole; the church is corporate unity. Paul's ethic involves the imperative and the indicative: "cleanse out the old leaven . . . as you really are unleavened." Become what you are! What they are is the result of God's action in Christ, "our paschal lamb" who "has been sacrificed." This Christological grounding of the ethical demand can become the basis for an effective sermon: it shows that the ethical life is a response to God's revelation in Christ—that Christ is the motive and norm for Christian conduct. In response to this revelation, the believer is called to joyous celebration. While the reference to celebrating the feast may allude to the Lord's Supper, Paul reminds the preacher that the whole of the Christian life is a celebration—a life "of sincerity and truth" (v. 8).

The problem of impurity within the church suggests the larger issue of the church in the world. Actually, Paul had written an earlier letter (see Intro.) which warned the believers not to associate with immoral people. He did not mean, as the Corinthians had supposed, the immoral of the world. That would have required the Christians to retreat from the world. Instead, as a sermon could point out, the church is called to faithful witness in and to the world. Paul had intended to advise disassociation with any one called brother (i.e. any member of the congregation) who was guilty of gross immorality. In regard to the "immoral of this world"—those outside the church—the Christians have no right now to judge; God will take care of that in an eschatological judgment. Nevertheless, believers, have a present responsibility to preserve the purity of the church. Paul's earlier advice, therefore, is to be heeded: the Corinthians should not have fellowship, including the eating of the Lord's Supper, with a person guilty of gross immorality. "Drive out the wicked person from among you" (v. 13). Stated homiletically, the church should not go out of the world, the world should go out of the church!

Why such drastic action? Isn't the church a haven for sinners? How are sinners to be redeemed apart from the influence of the church? Paul would probably answer that this is a particularly serious sin. More important, he would insist on the holiness of the church. To be sure, his view of the church as corporate unity is remote from modern church life where one can scarcely catch measles, let alone sin! Moreover, despite his lack of clarity, Paul is convinced that his advice will be good for both the church and the individual (whose spirit will be saved, v. 5). Most important, Paul is not suggesting that this man is the only sinner in the congregation, but that this gross sin is totally ignored—the Corinthians are proud. What is needed (then and now) is a conviction of sin—always the first step toward salvation. This conviction will not be realized in the comfortable climate of permissive indifference but in the concerned discipline of the redemptive fellowship. All of this reminds us of the ethical seriousness of Paul's religion—an ethical concern which demands relevance from our sermons. God requires righteousness; sin stands under his wrath (Rom 1:18); he calls his people to holiness.

Lawsuits and License (6:1–20)

The responsibility for judging those inside the church (5:12) suggests another problem: settling legal disputes among Christians. Apparently, members of the Corinthian church were taking their civil conflicts to the pagan courts for litigation. Paul's way of raising the question is already censorious: Does one "dare to go to law before the unrighteous" (i.e. the unbelievers) "instead of the saints" (i.e. the Christians)? Like the Jews, who made use of the synagogue courts, the believers should bring their disputes before the church. Paul's argument employs an apocalyptic motif: the saints will judge the world, even the angels (Dan 7:22). This concept, which

was taken up by early Christians (Matt 19:28), did not mean
that believers should judge outsiders now (5:12– 13), but that
they would share in the future judgment. Arguing from the
greater to the lesser, Paul observes that if they can participate
in that ultimate judgment, Christians ought to be able to "try
trivial cases" and to judge "matters pertaining to this life."
When such cases arise, they should not be taken before "men
who count for nothing in our community" (v. 4; NEB), that is,
pagan jurists. Instead, the Corinthians should find within the
congregation persons whose wisdom is adequate for judging
these cases. When Paul says, "Shame on you!" (TEV), he implies another argument: that airing these disputes before pagans is detrimental to the Christian witness—a public denial
of the gospel of love.

In v. 7 Paul shifts his argument to higher ground. "To
have lawsuits at all . . . is defeat for you." Rather than take a
brother or sister to court, the Christian should suffer wrong
and be defrauded (see Matt 5:39– 42). Indeed, within the
church there should be no cause for retaliation—no wronging
or defrauding in the first place. Yet, Paul like realists of all
times, has to recognize that Christians ignore the law of love
and wrong each other. In responding to this situation, Paul affirms an ethic of absolute and relative: the absolute is that
there should be no wronging and no retaliation; the relative is
that when there is wrongdoing, and where civil disputes arise,
settlement should be by the church according to Christian
precepts. When the relative principle operates, it continues to
stand under the demand of the absolute—wrongdoing is
wrong and retaliation is bad. Thus, a sermon on "situation
ethics" ought to draw the important distinction: the situation
does not determine the ethic; the law of love judges and redeems the situation.

The consideration of wrongdoing within the church
evokes a more general ethical discussion. To show the danger
of immorality in Corinth, Paul takes up a conventional hellenistic vice-list (vv. 9– 10). The Jews, under the influence of
Stoic ethics, used lists of this sort for moral instruction and
anti-pagan polemic. The details of the list are conventional,
designed to magnify the extent of pagan wrongdoing. On the
question of homosexuality (see Rom 1:26– 27), Paul is thor-
oughly Jewish. He does not, however, condemn the sexuality

of anyone, but decries what he considers sexual aberrations— fornication, adultery, and "homosexual perversion" (NEB). When Paul asserts, "Such were some of you," he does not necessarily mean that all of these evils had actually been practiced by members of the church, but that the Christians of Corinth had belonged to a society stained by immorality. All that has changed. The believers were washed, justified, sanctified—terms which describe the basic Christian experience and provide an outline for a sermon. That they were washed means that the believers had experienced baptism—a rite which rendered them dead to sin (Rom 6:1–11). That they were sanctified means that they had been set apart as holy— an act of God confirmed by the gift of the Spirit (1 Thess 4:7– 8). That they were justified means that they had been brought into right relationship with God—a relationship grounded in grace and received by faith (Rom 3:21–26). These verses remind the Corinthians of what they once were and what they now are. For us, they suggest a sermon about the "heirs of the kingdom"—sinners made saints by the grace of God.

The vice-list prompts Paul's return to the question of sexual morality. In v. 12, he considers a slogan of the Corinthians: "All things are lawful" (see 10:23). Apparently, some members of the congregation, inspired by Paul's doctrine of freedom (Gal 5:1,13), supposed that Christianity meant, "Anything goes!" Although Paul agrees with the basic meaning of the slogan, he qualifies the statement in two ways. Though all things are lawful, not all things are helpful, that is, some things do not serve "the common good" (12:7). Though all things are lawful, the Christians should not, like many modern devotees of license, be enslaved to freedom—an obvious homiletical theme! The distinction between authentic freedom and a freedom which enslaves is drawn by means of two illustrations: (1) food and the stomach; (2) immorality and the body. Apparently, the Corinthians considered appetite for food and craving for sex to be pretty much the same, and assumed that the satisfying of both was assured by Christian freedom.

While Paul accepts the argument about food, he denies the claim about sex. Food is for the stomach and the stomach is for food, and "God will destroy both" (v. 13). In other words, food serves a physical function; there is nothing ultimate about it. The body, on the other hand, is more than mere flesh. For "body," Paul uses the term *soma*—a word which can stand for the whole person. The body is not meant for sexual immorality, but belongs to the Lord. The bodies of the believers are members of Christ (12:27), and as God raised him, so he will raise them as spiritual bodies (15:44). Since the body, the self, belongs to Christ, it cannot be united with a prostitute. If a man has intercourse with a prostitute, he becomes one body with her. As the OT indicates (Gen 2:24), "The two will become one flesh" (v. 16; NASB). On the other hand, the one who is united with Christ "becomes one Spirit with him" (Rom 8:9–11; Gal 2:20). The point for preaching is that a perverse physical relationship can destroy a spiritual relationship, and the spiritual relationship with Christ is an exclusive relationship which involves the total person. The Christians should flee sexual immorality because it is a serious sort of sin. Perhaps the free spirits of Corinth are saying, "Every sin is outside the body"—that is, sin, like food, is a matter of indifference. For Paul, sexual immorality is different: it is not simply a physical matter; it concerns the whole person. As any perceptive moralist knows, sexual relationships involve more than sex! The basis for sexual morality is profound: Your body is "a temple of the Holy Spirit" (v. 19); like a Greek temple, the body is the dwelling of God. Freedom does not mean license, for "you were bought with a price" (see 7:23). Just as the slave's liberty can be purchased, so the believer's freedom has been bought at high cost—the death of Christ (Gal 4:1–7). The one who has been freed belongs to another master and lives in responsible obedience. The new freedom becomes the basis for an ethical imperative: "Glorify God in your body."

To Marry or Not to Marry
(1 Corinthians 7:1 – 40)

Paul turns to questions raised by the letter he has received from the Corinthians (see Intro.). The phrase "now concerning" (7:25; 8:1; 12:1) is a shorthand way to refer to "matters about which you wrote." Like many moderns, the Corinthians were concerned about sex and marriage. Paul deals with the questions frankly—sex is not to be given the silent treatment. Probably there were a variety of opinions within the church, running all the way from tolerance of sexual license (6:13 – 18) to promotion of sexual asceticism. The statement "It is well for a man not to touch a woman" (v. 1) may be a slogan of the ascetics. In any case, Paul appears to sympathize with their position. Throughout the chapter he expresses preference for celibacy (vv. 26, 32, 38, 40) and uses his own behavior as an example (vv. 7, 8).

Paul's reasons for this preference, I think, are his mistaken eschatology (7:25 – 31) and his restricted view of marriage (7:32 – 35). Actually, Paul appears to have abandoned his Jewish heritage which considered marriage a duty grounded in divine command (Gen 2:18). In spite of his preference, Paul permits marriage as a concession. The concession is granted "because of the temptation to immorality" (v. 2). That is, marriage is to be allowed for those who cannot remain continent; some people have a gift for celibacy, some don't. For those who do not have the gift, sexual needs are to be fulfilled within a monogamous relationship. Within that relationship, intercourse is to be practiced with mutual consideration. Paul's claim that "the husband does not rule over his own body, but the wife does" (v. 4) must have come as a shock to many of his contemporaries as it does to male chauvinists today. Sexual abstinence for religious purposes may be observed by mutual consent, but only for a time. Then, the temptation to extramarital sex is to be overcome by sexual gratification within marriage. Essentially the same advice is given to the unmarried (perhaps, "widowers") and widows (vv. 8 – 9). Though it would be better for them to remain as Paul (a widower?), it is better to marry than to burn with sexual passion.

On the question of divorce, Paul knows a command of the Lord "that the wife should not separate from her husband" (v. 10). He is familiar with traditional words of Jesus like those later recorded in Mark 10:2 – 12. According to Jewish law, wives could not instigate divorce proceedings. Paul's appeal to Christ's authority makes the exception clause ("but if she does," v. 11) all the more surprising. Again, Paul presents the principle of the absolute and the relative (see 6:7 – 8)—a principle which has important implications for our preaching. Like most of us, Paul had learned that maintaining an absolute position on this matter is virtually impossible, even ill-advised. Some marriages are mistaken from the start, and the valiant effort to preserve a mismatch may make matters worse. Nevertheless, Paul's citation of the word of the Lord (the absolute) serves to underscore the seriousness of the separation (the relative) and to indicate that divorce stands under judgment. Even after this point is acknowledged, however, I find it difficult to agree with Paul's application of the relative—that the woman "remain single or else be reconciled to her husband" (v. 11). Does not the forgiveness of God provide the possibility of a Christian marriage?

In regard to "mixed marriages" Paul has no instruction from the Lord. Jesus did not deal with the sort of situation which had arisen at Corinth—a situation in which one partner of a marriage had joined the Christian community and the other had remained a pagan. Paul advises maintaining such a marriage, though the consent of the non-believer is required. His reason for this advice is that the unbelieving partner is sanctified through the believing spouse. That is, the consecrating grace of God can function through the intimacy of a marriage (contrast 6:16). Proof of this sanctifying power of marriage is seen in its fruit—children who are recognized as holy. Contrary to the claims of some of his critics, Paul affirms a high view of marriage and a profound understanding of family solidarity which can inform our preaching. Nevertheless, the pagan partner should be allowed to separate. Beyond this, I find the rest of vv. 15 – 16 unclear. It is not certain whether God's call to peace means to maintain the marriage or to let it be dissolved; and it is not clear whether the (meager) prospects of converting the spouse are to encourage separation or to maintain the marriage.

Paul's instruction about mixed marriage leads to a more general maxim: "each one . . . should continue as he was when God's call reached him" (v. 17, JB)—advice repeated at the end of the paragraph (v. 24). Paul's point (which could be developed into an effective sermon) is that the call of God has come to people in their particular situation, and that the call comes by God's grace rather than by human accomplishment. The point is clarified by two illustrations. First, Paul suggests that those circumcised at the time of their call should not seek to remove the marks of circumcision (see 1 Macc 1:15), and that those who were uncircumcised when they became believers should not seek to be circumcised (see Gal 6:12–13). This is because neither circumcision nor uncircumcision "counts for anything" (see Gal 5:6); what counts is "keeping the commandments of God" (v. 19). Paul's hearers might have been confounded by this conclusion; circumcision is a command of God, as Gen 17:10–14 makes clear! Paul, however, has a different understanding of obedience. Not only does he replace the ritual with the ethical, he views the external as mere sign of the more basic, inner commitment (Rom 2:29).

In his second illustration, Paul says that a person who was a slave when called need not worry about that. The meaning of v. 21b, however, is hotly debated. Some interpreters think Paul is urging the slave to seize the opportunity for freedom, while others believe he is encouraging the slave to remain in slavery. In context, the latter interpretation seems better, for one is to "remain in the state in which he was called" (v. 20). Actually, the decision for the freeing of a slave rested with the master; the slave had little to say about the matter. In any event, Paul's point is that the Christian whether slave or free should live in obedience to the new master, the Lord Jesus Christ. Paul's advice here should not be read as blanket approval of slavery. Rather than affirming the status quo, Paul believed the world was under the control of evil forces (Rom 8:38; 1 Cor 2:8; 2 Cor 4:4)—forces which God was about to destroy (15:24). The believers already anticipate the life of the new age (2 Cor 5:17): though slaves, they are truly free (Gal 5:1); though free, they are truly slaves of Christ (Rom 1:1; Gal 1:10). Just as slaves could be freed by a costly payment, so Christians were "bought with a price" (v. 23; 6:20)—the sacrifice of Christ.

As a preacher, I have wrestled with the theme: the paradox of slavery and freedom. It is easy to understand how some who suppose they are free are actually slaves—even slaves of the things that make them free. It is much more difficult to affirm that those who are enslaved—in situations of injustice or poverty—are truly free. Doesn't this affirmation purchase cheap inwardness at the price of genuine freedom? Yet, Paul's advice was not designed to salve the conscience of the master nor quench the hope of the slave. It was intended to put the matter in a larger framework—to urge that true freedom can never be attained by human effort. To focus exclusively on programs of social change—even those demanded by the gospel—is to look to things which are seen, not to the eternal (2 Cor 4:18). True freedom has to do with the ultimate, with one's relation to God.

In vv. 25–35, Paul presents reasons for preferring celibacy. His first reason is eschatological: one should remain single "in view of the impending distress" (v. 26). The woes of the end-time are bad enough without the complicating cares of marriage and family (see Mark 13:17). Since "the appointed time has grown very short" (v. 29), one should avoid any disruptive change, seeking neither to marry nor to be free from marriage. Yet, marriage is to be allowed, and, though ill-advised, not viewed as sin. Since "the form of this world is passing away" (v. 31), the believer ought to live in freedom from the transient structure of worldly existence. Of course, when Paul says, "let those who have wives live as though they had none" (v. 29), he does not mean that married persons should ignore the responsibilities of marriage (7:2–5); and when he says that those who mourn or rejoice should live as though not mourning nor rejoicing, Paul does not mean that Christians should neither mourn nor rejoice, nor sympathize with those who do (Rom 12:15). Instead, as a sermon could indicate, Paul means that believers should live in the freedom of the new creation (2 Cor 5:17), not captive to the temporary and the transcient, "not conformed to this world" (Rom 12:2).

Paul's second reason for preferring celibacy rests on a restricted view of marriage. He believes the unmarried person is anxious about the affairs of the Lord and is concerned to please the Lord. The married person, on the other hand, is preoccupied with wordly affairs and is anxious to please the spouse. This idyllic picture of husbands and wives busily engaged in spouse-pleasing is ground enough to argue that Paul had never been married! But, more seriously, Paul should have known that plenty of unmarried people were anxious about a lot of things besides the affairs of the Lord. He seems to have been oblivious to a possibility which a sermon could point out—that within a Christian marriage "undivided devotion to the Lord" (v. 35) could be fully achieved.

No one knows for sure whom Paul is addressing in vv. 36–38. There are three main theories: (1) he is giving advice to a Christian father about his virgin daughter (NASB); (2) he is instructing engaged Christians about marriage (RSV); (3) he is speaking to couples living in "spiritual marriage"—a marriage where man and woman live together without sexual relations (NEB). Regardless of the details of interpretation, Paul's basic advice is clear: celibacy is preferred, but the consummation of a marriage is allowed for those who cannot control their sexual desires. Essentially the same advice is offered in vv. 39–40. When the husband dies, the wife is free to marry, though "only in the Lord," that is, only to another member of the Christian community. Yet, like others addressed in the chapter, the widow will be happier if she remains single. Though Paul is proud of his authority (2 Cor 10:8), he, as every faithful minister, knows that judgments are necessary where divine sanctions are not readily available. In making such judgments Paul hopes he has the spirit of God.

To Eat or Not to Eat
(1 Corinthians 8:1 – 11:1)

Food Offered to Idols (8:1 – 13)

Paul turns to another question raised by the Corinthian letter: Can a Christian eat meat which has been offered to a pagan idol?—a question taken up again in 10:14. While it may seem trivial to us, this was a matter of serious dispute within the church. Much of the meat sold in the Corinthian market had been sacrificed to pagan deities. To eat such meat was strictly forbidden by the Jews—a view shared by some conservatives in the early church (Acts 15:29). The opposite position—that one could eat such meat—was advocated by the liberals of Corinth.

Resolution of the problem was important to the life of the church, since its central act of worship, the Lord's Supper, involved the eating of a meal (see 11:25). In v. 1, Paul probably cites a slogan of the liberals: "all of us possess knowledge." According to this knowledge, "an idol has no real existence" and "there is no God but one" (v. 4). Yet Paul, while agreeing, insists that this knowledge "puffs up"; it encourages the kind of arrogance which characterizes the style of many of the Corinthians (4:6, 18, 19; 5:2). Love, on the other hand, "builds up"; it fosters the kind of mutual concern which edifies the Christian community (10:23; 14:3, 5, 12). An interesting sermon could be preached, I believe, on the theme: "love and knowledge." The Corinthian intellectuals imagine they know something, while in fact they lack authentic knowledge of God (see 1:21). The true way to knowledge is to abandon egocentric striving in favor of humble commitment. "If one loves God (2:9; Rom 8:28) one is known by him" (v. 3; see Gal 4:9). This strange twist in the argument shows that love is superior to knowledge and that God cannot be conceived as the object of human inquiry. The little mind of man cannot encompass the transcendent God. We know him because he first knows us (see 1 John 4:19) and makes himself known in Jesus Christ. In response to this revelation, we love God and acknowledge that we are known by him; knowledge of God is realized in personal experience.

To show how knowledge of God is grounded in commitment, Paul quotes an early Christian creed—perhaps a confession recited at baptism. This confession provides a text for extensive preaching on the doctrine of God and Christology. Although there may be many so-called gods, "for us there is one God" (v. 6). This affirmation does not deny the existence of other spiritual forces—principalities, powers (Rom 8:38), demons (10:20)—but insists that theology must be confessional—"for us." About God, three things are affirmed: he is Father (intimately related to his people, Gal 4:6); he is Creator (the source of all things); he is Redeemer (the origin and destiny of the new creation). For Christ, the confession uses the title "Lord"—the same term which the Greek translation of the OT uses for Yahweh. This Lord is the means *through* whom God created all things and *through* whom God effected the new creation.

The question which comes to my mind is, How can Paul confess one God *and* "one Lord, Jesus Christ"? Has Christianity compromised Paul's monotheism? To be sure, Paul appears to posit a subordination Christology (see 15:28) in his distinction between God the cause and Christ the means. Yet, Paul is not primarily concerned with questions which occupied later Christological controversy—the nature of Christ or his metaphysical relation to God. Paul affirms a functional Christology—that God acts through Christ, that the creative and redemptive power of God is uniquely present in the one we confess as Lord. In context, this confession denies that an idol has real existence, that an idol can taint meat, and that food created by God can be called taboo (see 10:26).

Not all the Corinthians, however, share this knowledge. Some who have been steeped in idolatry, cannot get it out of their heads that sacrificial meat is tainted. If they eat, their consciences are defiled. To those who know that idols have no power, Paul points out that food cannot commend them to God (see Rom 14:13– 23). They are no worse off by not eating, nor better off by eating—alternatives available to the intellectuals. They, unlike the weaker members, are free not to eat or to eat; they are free and responsible. Apparently the Corinthi-

an liberals considered eating to be a badge of their Christian
freedom. This freedom, however, could become a cause of
stumbling for the weak. When they see one of the knowledgea-
ble "at table in an idol's temple" (perhaps at a restaurant in a
temple area; participation in cultic meals was forbidden; see
10:21), they might be encouraged to eat and violate their consciences. If this example of eating should cause one of the
weak to fall, Paul declares, "I will never eat meat" (v. 13).

I find Paul's argument to provide a profound basis for ethical preaching. An act which is not wrong in itself (see 10:25,
27) is designated sin—against one's brethren and sin against
Christ. In Christian ethics, persons are more important than
precepts. Moreover, this concern for persons is measured by
Christological dimensions. In our time, many programs for
good are moved by a concern for humanity—by a concern to
recognize persons as heirs of basic human rights. To programs
of this sort, under whatever banner, Christians should say,
Amen! The Christian ethic, however, is still more profoundly
based. Why is the brother or sister important?—because he or
she is the person "for whom Christ died" (v. 11).

Support for Ministers (9:1–27)

Having argued that one can forgo one's rights in alle-
giance to a higher principle, Paul proceeds to illustrate the
point by an example from his own ministry. He begins by ask-
ing, "Am I not free? Am I not an apostle?" By this he means
that as an apostle (1:1) he is free to claim the rights of an apostle. Among these rights are the right to food and drink, the
right to be accompanied by a wife, and the right to refrain
from self-support. When I read of apostles accompanied by
wives, I conjure up visions of "house trailer evangelists"
whose spouses inspire the auditors with vibra-harps and
chalk-talks. What role the wives played in the apostolic mission, of course, remains a mystery, but apparently some of the
preachers like Cephas (Peter) and the brothers of the Lord
(Mark 3:31; 6:3; Gal 1:19) took their wives along.

To make a case for ministerial support Paul cites an analogy: "Who serves as a soldier at his own expense?" (v. 7). If the
troops of the emperor deserve to be paid, so also the soldiers of
Christ. Two additional questions employ the same sort of argument: "Who plants a vineyard and does not eat of its

grapes? Who tends a flock and does not drink of the milk?"
(NIV). The meaning is self-evident: just as a farmer or herds-
man is entitled to a share of the fruits of his labor, so the minister has a right to expect support from the church.

Beyond these analogies, Paul attempts to ground his argument in Scripture. He cites Deut 25:4: "You shall not muz-
zle an ox when it treads out the grain"; that is, as the ox is
tramping around the threshing floor it is to be allowed a
mouthful of grain now and then. To me, Paul's exegesis is far-
fetched. When he asks, "God is not concerned for oxen, is He?"
(v. 9; NASB), Paul expects a negative answer. The point of the
text (and the basis for an ecology sermon) is precisely the opposite: God *is* concerned for his creation, including oxen.
When Paul goes on to ask, "Does he not speak entirely for our
sake?", the answer, contrary to Paul's expectation, is "No!"
God did *not* have the early Christian preachers in view. Apparently, the apostle reads the Deuteronomy text as having a
broader meaning—as referring to the whole process of plow-
ing and threshing. Thus, the person who plows and the person
who threshes have a hope of sharing in the crop. In the same
way, the minister who has sown spiritual things ought to be
able to reap "material benefits"—a valid point in spite of the
exegesis.

Paul concludes that he has not made use of this right to
ministerial support (see vv. 15–18). He forgoes support because he does not want to "put an obstacle in the way of the
gospel" (v. 12; see v. 23). Perhaps Paul wants to avoid the
charge that he, like popular public speakers of the hellenistic
age (or some affluent evangelists of our time), is preaching for
personal gain (see 2 Cor 2:17). At this point another argument
occurs to Paul which makes use of both Scripture and analogy, and has to do with persons actually engaged in religious
service. "Those who perform the temple service eat the temple
offerings, and those who wait upon the altar claim their share
of the sacrifice" (v. 13; NEB; see Num 18:8, 31). This OT point
is buttressed by a traditional word of Jesus to the effect that
"those who preach the gospel should receive their living from
the gospel" (NIV; see Luke 10:7). I would agree, and urge ministers to display less false modesty in their budget raising sermons; preachers deserve to be paid! Paul, nevertheless, has
"made no use of any of these rights" (v. 15), and is not writing

to secure them. He renounces these rights because he does not want to be deprived of his "ground for boasting." Paul's boasting is not, as one might suppose, his preaching; he preaches out of necessity. "Woe to me if I do not preach the gospel" (v. 16). This is an excellent text for a sermon to preachers who need to remember that their preaching is motivated by the compulsion of the divine commission (see Amos 3:8). Paul's argument assumes that one can only boast about what one does voluntarily. As he says, "If I had chosen this work myself, I might have been paid for it" (v. 17; JB). What he does of his own free will is to preach the gospel "free of charge." Thus, he foregoes the right to pay so that he may have another sort of reward. We need to be reminded, too, that in spite of the needs for adequate ministerial compensation, the right to preach bears its own reward.

Refusing support is symbolic of a larger ministerial method (vv. 19–23). The basic principle is set forth in v. 19: "Though I am free from all men, I have made myself a slave to all, that I might win the more." The principle—being free (v. 1; Gal 5:1), yet accepting slavery (2 Cor 4:5) in order to win people—is developed by reference to various groups. To the Jews, Paul becomes as a Jew—that is, he associates with Jews—in the conduct of ministry. He does this in order to win Jews to the faith (see Rom 11:13–14). In the next clause, he refers to the Jews as "those under the law." Though free from the law (Rom 7:4–6; 10:4), Paul can become as "one under the law"; he can choose to obey the precepts of the law, for they are holy, righteous and good (Rom 7:12). Yet, Paul adds a qualifying parenthesis: "though not being myself under the law" (v. 20). The law as external, legalistic system of salvation cannot be imposed upon him. To those outside the law (the Gentiles), Paul can become as one outside the law—that is, he can associate with Greeks and Romans. But again, a qualifying parenthesis is added: "not being without law toward God but under the law of Christ" (v. 21). Although he does not recognize the law as determining his relationship to God, Paul has not abandoned obedience. Rather than being without law, he is under the new law, the "law of Christ" (Gal 6:2; Rom 8:2). This law is no law at all in the ordinary legal sense, yet it is more demanding than any code carved on the stones of human history. This suggests a sermon on the theme, "Freedom from Law and the Law of Christ"—the law of love.

Next Paul says, "To the weak I became weak" (v. 22)—referring to the weak brethren of 8:7– 13. Although he shares the knowledge of the Corinthian intellectuals, Paul is willing to become weak (give up his right to eat sacrificial food) in order to win the weak. What does it mean to win the weak? Of course, it could mean to win them to a stronger conscience—educate them to a more sophisticated theology. I am more inclined to believe, however, that winning the weak means to save them from the arrogance of those who can destroy (8:11).

Finally, Paul repeats his general principle: "I have become all things to all men" (v. 22)—a much maligned text. To become all things to all people does not mean to do your own thing any time or place; it does not suggest that the minister become a moral chameleon, changing color to match the context. Paul becomes all things in order to save some; his freedom is limited by a higher purpose. The criterion for the total conduct of ministry is the message which saves. As Paul says in v. 23, "I do it all for the sake of the gospel."

The demands of the gospel suggest a discussion of discipline—a concern especially appropriate for the Corinthians and lax Christians of every age. Here Paul makes use of metaphors drawn from the arena. This was a favorite source of illustrations for hellenistic authors, and a likely location for sermon topics in our age of superbowls and superstars. Paul's readers no doubt thought of the Isthmian games, held every second year in a Corinthian suburb. Paul reminds them that in the stadium, all the runners compete, but only one receives a prize. On the basis of this obvious fact, Paul urges the Corinthians to run (to conduct their lives) so as to obtain the prize. What it takes to be a winner is arduous training—the sort of self-discipline demanded of good athletes. While athletes strive to win a "perishable wreath," the goal of the Christian is imperishable—salvation, new life with God, "the crown of righteousness" (2 Tim 4:8).

On the surface of it, the picture of Christians as "winners" who obtain salvation by heroic effort does not seem entirely consistent with the gospel of grace and faith. Yet, Paul is correct in his conviction that faith is responsible and obedience

demands effort—that one must "press on toward the goal for
the prize of the upward call of God" (Phil 3:14). In this understanding, Paul says, "I run straight for the finish line" (v. 26;
TEV). This need for discipline is even more demanding in box-
ing. Paul does not beat the air, but pommels his body—the
Greek word can mean "give a black eye." This shows that the
way to victory is the way of sacrifice, and suggests the theme:
"Crown and Cross." If Paul fails to exercise this kind of rigor
in his ministry, he, like the undisciplined athlete, may be dis-
qualified. If Paul can fall away, how much more the undisciplined Christians of every age.

The Table of the Lord and the Table of Demons (10:1–11:1)

Paul returns to the question of meat offered to idols. First,
he draws a distinction between eating sacrificial food and
worshiping idols. Participation in pagan culture makes idolatry a persistent threat—even to those who have experienced
the benefits of Christian rites. To make his case, Paul employs
typology, that is, he interprets OT incidents as instructional
examples for the church. Passing through the sea (Exod 14:22)
and traveling under the cloud (Exod 13:21) are viewed as
"types" of baptism, and eating "supernatural food" (the manna of Exod 16:4) and drinking "supernatural drink" (Num
20:11) are viewed as prefiguring the Lord's Supper. Supernatural drink had been provided from the rock at Kadesh (Num
20:10–13). The rabbis, noting the later reference to God's provision of water (Num 21:16), imagined that water throughout
the wilderness wandering was dispensed from this awesome
rock—am ambulatory rock "which followed them" (v. 4).

When Paul says, "the Rock was Christ" (v. 4), I don't think
he was positing a high-flown doctrine of preexistence. More
likely, he viewed the rock as a "type" of Christ—a sign of the
life-giving power of God manifest in God's care for Israel and
realized in the gift of Jesus Christ. In any case, Paul's basic
meaning is clear: the Israelites experienced the grace of God
in events which prefigure baptism and the Lord's Supper,
and, just as "God was not pleased" with their subsequent behavior ("the desert was strewn with their corpses," v. 5, NEB),
so Corinthian participation in baptism and the Lord's Supper
is no guarantee that they will not be "overthrown in the wil-

derness" of their pagan environment. There is a sermon here: "Sacramental Grace and Moral Responsibility."

Next, Paul presents examples of how Israel, though favored by God's grace, had fallen into idolatry and immorality—"warnings for us" (v. 6). First, he cites the incident of the golden calf where the people "sat down to eat and drink" and arose to pagan revelry (Exod 32:6). Next, he mentions the plague which was visited upon the people because they played the harlot with the daughters of Moab and ate the sacrifices to their gods (Num 25:9). (Although the text in Numbers reports that 24,000 were killed, Paul's 23,000 may represent confusion with the 3,000 of Exod 32:28.) The reference to serpents remembers the fiery snakes of Num 21:6. Grumbling was characteristic of the wandering people, but Paul may have in mind the murmuring punished by a destructive plague (Num 16:41–50). Engaging in a sort of existential exegesis, Paul says "these things . . . were written down for our instruction, upon whom the end of the ages has come"—a provocative text.

Christians yesterday and today live in the time of fulfillment, for they are heirs of the instructive history of the people of God. Like the Israelites and the Corinthians the modern heirs of God's gifts can be lured into an easy security or plagued by spiritual arrogance. "Let any one who thinks that he stands take heed lest he fall" (v. 12) is the sermon's text. Do not suppose that you will avoid the temptations which are common to humanity; do not imagine that your temptations are unique. Yet, for all the universality of temptation, the believer can endure. A way of escape will be provided, for the God who judges our easy security and spiritual arrogance remains faithful.

The reason believers must "flee from idolatry" (v. 14; NIV) is the exclusive character of Christian worship—another homiletical theme. Most people are not monotheists, consistently worshiping the God who made heaven and earth, but henotheists who serve various idols on different occasions— job, family, social acceptance, and on Sunday, the Father of Jesus Christ. Judgment on that is declared in the central act of worship, the Lord's Supper. The "cup of blessing" (i.e. the cup over which thanksgiving has been offered; Mark 14:23) symbolizes participation in the blood of Christ. Partaking of the

cup involves an exclusive relation to Christ—sharing his suffering (Phil 3:10), participating in his death (Rom 6:3– 4). The
bread broken in the simple ritual of the Supper signifies a
share in the body of Christ (12:27)—the church which has a
distinctive relation to the Lord. Since there is "one loaf," the
believers, though many, are "one body." Thus, the bread represents both the unity with Christ and the oneness of the community of faith.

In the cultic life of Israel, the priests who ate of the sacrifices shared a relation to the altar (Lev 7:6: 10:12– 15). This
OT illustration has implications for the question of meat offered to idols. It does not imply that "an idol is anything" (v.
19), but than an idol which "has no real existence" (8:4) represents a demon. The worship of images made by the hands or
minds of people is not simply worship of nothing, it is dedica-
tion to demonic power. Therefore, Christian worship, unlike
the contemporary cults of the ancient and modern world, is
exclusive and non-syncretistic: "You cannot partake of the table of the Lord and the table of demons" (v. 21). Failure to
obey this admonition will "provoke the Lord to jealously"—a
frequent OT theme (Deut 32:16) and an appropriate warning
to the spiritually arrogant (4:8). A variety of communion sermons are suggested by this text: "one loaf, one body" (Christian unity), "the altar and holiness" (sacrament and ethics),
"table of the Lord and table of demons" (Christian worship
against secular syncretism).

Having demonstrated the distinctive character of Christian worship. Paul proceeds to the specific question of food offered to idols. The slogan of the intellectuals (already cited in
6:12) is repeated and explicated with minor variation. Although "all things are lawful," all things are not helpful (as he
said before) and "not all things build up" (v. 23). The new element, building up, probably means building up the church
(Rom 14:19), and, in particular, seeking the good of the fellow-
Christian (Rom 15:2). Because all things are lawful, the believer can "eat whatever is sold in the meat market"—a conclusion based not only on Christian freedom, but also on the
doctrine of creation. Since "the earth is the Lord's," everything in it belongs to him and is essentially good (Gen 1:31).
Just as one can buy freely at the market, so the Christian—no
hothouse ascetic—can accept an invitation to a pagan dinner

party and eat whatever is served. Christian liberty must not be restricted by the over-scrupulous who are always out to shackle someone else's freedom (v. 29b). If one can say grace over the food, says Paul, it is OK to eat (Rom 14:6).

Vv. 28–29a (which I take with the RSV as a parenthesis) notes the exception to this freedom and shows (as 8:7–13) how one must "seek the good" of the neighbor (v. 24). If someone points out that the food has been offered in sacrifice, then, out of consideration for the informer's conscience (8:10), the believer should say, "No thanks, please pass the potatoes!" This vacillating advice—that sometimes you eat and sometimes you don't—provides another occasion to address the popular fascination with "situation ethics" (see on 6:7–8). Paul seems sympathetic to the approach in his advice to do different (even opposite) things in different contexts. He certainly does not think that the Christian ethic is a rigid set of rules, but that it has its meaning in situations of life where simple right-and-wrongs are often difficult to discern. In no case, however, does Paul assume that the ethical imperative is determined by the situation. The ethic is moved by concern for the brother, and the brother or sister is the person "for whom Christ died" (8:11). Christ is the norm for Christian conduct.

A similar point is made in Paul's conclusion: "Whatever you do, do all to the glory of God" (v. 31; see 7:35). In all our conduct, we are responsible to the ultimate—to the God whose will is revealed in Christ. Just as Paul can become all things to all people (9:22), so also he intends to give no offense to anyone—Jews, Greeks, or the church. Members of the community of faith should "command the respect" of insider and outsider alike (1 Thess 4:12). Paul does not try to please everybody in order to gain advantage for himself; he seeks the advantage "of the many, that they may be saved" (v. 33). Any picture of Paul as a fawning people-pleaser is out of focus (see 1 Cor 4:12–13 and 2 Cor 11:24–28); Paul didn't get thrown into prison for winning popularity contests. This is why imitating Paul, though a model for communicating salvation, is not an exercise in pleasing the public. Indeed, to imitate Paul is to conform to a higher norm: "Be imitators of me, as I am of Christ" (11:1).

A sermon on imitating Christ should be developed with

caution. There is a sense in which Christ cannot be imitated—e.g. his unique role in God's revelatory and redemptive purpose. What Paul has in mind is not primarily the moral example of Jesus of Nazareth, but the obedient condescension of the incarnate one—the one who "emptied himself, taking the form of a servant" (Phil 2:7– 8). To imitate Christ means to embody the love of God in the life of the believer and in the program of the church.

Ways to Worship
(1 Corinthians 11:2 – 14:40)

Women with Veils (11:2 – 16)

In chaps. 11 – 14, Paul takes up a question which has bothered the church since its inception: How to worship. If even the disciples who had left home and job to follow Jesus asked, "Lord, teach us to pray" (Luke 11:1), how much more Christians in every age have been baffled by the problem of worship. The preacher will be baffled, too, when trying to make sense out of Paul's discussion of veils. Regardless of the difficulties, the question of veils has to do with traditional practice in the church (vv. 2, 16) and is related to decorum in the conduct of public worship. The excesses of Corinthian enthusiasm may have been especially characteristic of the women (see on 12:2), who like some of their contemporaries, were tossing away their veils as a mark of feminist liberation.

In v. 3, Paul sets out his basic principle: a cosmic order exists in which Christ is the head of man, man he head of woman, and God the head of Christ. This means that women are subordinate. The principle is supported by Paul's reading of Gen 2:18 – 23. There it is clear that woman was created to be a helper "for man," and that woman was made from a rib which had been taken "from man." Since man is the "head," he should not cover his "head" (a play on words). He is created in God's image (Gen 1:26) and reflects the divine glory. Since she is subordinate, the woman ought to wear a veil. She is created from man and reflects his glory.

Apparently, Paul has skipped over Gen 1:27, which indicates that both male and female were created in the image of God. It is also not clear to me how neglecting to wear a veil dishonors a woman's head, or how failure to wear a veil is the same as being shaven—especially since a woman's hair "is given to her for a covering" (v. 15). When Paul goes on to say that a woman ought to have "a sign of authority" (v. 10; NEB) on her head "because of the angels," nobody knows for sure what he means. Most likely, Paul is still pursuing his argument from natural order. He shared the worldview of most of his contemporaries which considered the angels to be the protectors of the order of the cosmos.

In vv. 11–12—which the RSV properly takes as a parenthesis—Paul almost redeems himself. Here he returns to the principle of mutuality which had characterized some of his remarks about marriage (7:4, 12–14). "Woman is not independent of man nor man of woman; for as woman was made from man, so man is now born of woman." Notice how Paul prefaces these statements with the phrase, "in the Lord." This seems to suggest that for those who are in the new situation of faith, the distinctions of the old order no longer count (see Gal 3:28). In the new age and from the new perspective, relationships are not determined by social custom but in response to the ultimate—"all things are from God" (v. 12).

But why, then, does Paul demand conformity to the styles of his culture in the worship of the church? Apparently, he believes that the social order ought to be respected in matters of custom—that insignificant details of decorum should give offense to no one (10:32). At any rate, the argument from contemporary custom claims the day. Surely custom, more than nature, teaches that men should wear short hair and women long. Finally, Paul appears to be frustrated with his own arguments. At the end of the matter, he simply pounds the pulpit: "We recognize no other practice!" (v. 16).

Except for vv. 11–12, I do not find much to preach about in this text. As a matter of fact, too much preaching has used these verses in a misplaced effort to retard the rights of women and dictate crew-cuts for men. Nevertheless, an important point can be made about biblical ethics—though in the negative. It is a mistake to try to apply the Bible's advice on particular issues to modern problems which seem superficially parallel. Paul's opinion on hair-styles—addressed to a totally different culture—is hardly normative for Christians today. The real question is: How does Paul's basic ethical commitment inform moral decisions in a decisively different cultural situation? If Paul were to answer that question christologically, as he usually does (5:7; 6:20; 8:11), he might say, veils are nothing, hair styles are nothing; "the only thing that counts is new creation!" (Gal 6:15; NEB).

The Supper According to Tradition (11:17– 34)

The central element of worship was the observance of the Lord's Supper; it was the primary reason for coming together (v. 33). Although he had commended the Corinthians on other matters (11:2), Paul was not able to praise their practice of the Supper (v. 17, 22). As a matter of fact, "your meetings for worship actually do more harm than good" (TEV)—an observation which ought to give pause to program planners in every age! The problem in serious: There are divisions at the table of the Lord. Paul uses two words to describe them: in v. 18 he speaks of *schismata* (schisms) and in v. 19 *haireseis* (heresies or factions). These schisms (the same word is used in 1:10) seem to be different from those mentioned in chap. 1. There they involved loyalty to leaders, while here they have to do with social and economic factors (vv. 21– 22).

Paul has heard about these divisions and partly believes it; rumors in the church should always be swallowed with a grain of salt! The parenthetical phrase—"dissensions are necessary if only to show which of your members are sound" (v. 19; NEB)—expresses irony; Paul does not believe that factions serve some good purpose. Indeed, the factions destroy the Supper. The Corinthians eat—the Supper involved a full meal (v. 25)—but they do not eat the Supper of the Lord. Rather than eating the Lord's Supper, "each of you goes ahead without waiting for anybody else" (v. 21; NIV). Proud individualism, typical of the Corinthians (4:6, 18; 5:2; 8:1), has turned the Supper into an exercise in private piety. The result is that "one is hungry and another is drunk" (v. 21). Those who are hungry probably represent the lower classes (1:26)—common laborers and slaves—who arrive late and go away empty. Those who are drunk may be the leisure class who can come early—who don't need sustenance and have plenty to eat at home. The Supper, though not an ordinary meal, is a real meal which meets physical needs. Failure to meet this need, and failure to observe the Supper in the unity of the community, is to "humiliate those who have nothing" and "despise the church of God."

To correct the Corinthians, Paul reminds them of the tradition of the Supper. When he says, "I received from the Lord what I also delivered to you" (v. 23), Paul is using technical

words for receiving and handing on tradition. The tradition
goes ultimately back to Jesus himself, who instituted the Supper "on the night when he was betrayed"—a solemn occasion
compared with Corinthian revelry. The Supper has its meaning in the context of the death of Jesus, and its celebration
stresses his action. Like a host at a Jewish meal, Jesus took
bread, gave thanks, and broke it. In interpreting his action,
Jesus said, "This is my body which is broken for you." The
breaking of the bread represents the offering of the life of
Jesus for his followers (15:3; Rom 3:25). In 5:7, Paul has described the death of Christ as the sacrifice of the paschal
lamb—a sacrifice which provides freedom from bondage. In
describing the second act of the ritual (after supper), Paul does
not say that the wine is Christ's blood (see 10:16), but that
"the cup is the new covenant" in his blood. Just as the old covenant was ratified by sacrifice (Exod 24:8), so the new agreement between God and his people (Jer 31:31 – 33) is confirmed
by the death of Christ, the supreme expression of God's love.

The Supper, according to the tradition, is to be repeated—observed again and again in remembrance of Christ. According to the ancient mind, to remember something was not
simply to recall it; to do something in remembrance was to
make the remembered event present. To the tradition, Paul
adds a comment of his own: "As often as you eat the bread and
drink the cup, you proclaim the Lord's death" (v. 26). The
Supper is proclamation; it represents the event of God's redemptive action in Christ. The observance of the Supper,
though it looks back to Christ's death, and though it remembers and realizes his presence, also looks forward to his coming (15:23). The celebration of the Supper is accompanied by
the cry of hope, "Our Lord, come!" (16:22).

Chastened by the tradition, the Corinthians must give attention to their own observance. Whoever eats and drinks "in
an unworthy manner, shall be guilty of the body and blood of
the Lord" (v. 27; NASB). Eating in an unworthy manner no
doubt refers to the practice Paul has censured in vv. 21 – 22 —
going ahead with one's meal and getting drunk at the table of
the Lord. Just as that action despises the church, so it also
puts one into opposition with the Lord of the church—identi-
fies one with the crucifiers of Jesus. Although the Supper is
not a private matter, it demands personal responsibility. The

participants must engage in self-examination to see if they are honoring the church and remaining faithful to the tradition. By careful judgment of themselves, they may hope to deflect the stern judgment of the Lord; but if they are judged by him, his judgment will provide the kind of discipline which can save them from ultimate condemnation (vv. 31–32). To eat and drink without "discerning the body" (v. 29) is to bring judgment on one's self.

Some interpreters suppose that discerning the body means to recognize that the body of the eucharist is the body of Christ—that there is a sacramental reality in the elements of the Supper which can cause some to be "weak and ill," and some to die. More in accord with the context, discerning the body means to recognize the church as the body of Christ (12:27)—means that participation in the unity of the community belongs to the essence of the Supper. Paul's concluding admonition has nothing to do with the theology of the eucharistic elements, but with the nature of the church. "When you come together to eat, wait for one another."

There are enough sermons and communion meditations in this text to keep the preacher busy for a long time: the Supper and unity—all classes of people sit together at the table of the Lord; the Supper as a full meal though not an ordinary meal—worship has physical as well as spiritual meaning; worship as vital tradition rather than habitual custom; the Supper as memory, presence, and hope (three points!); Lord's Supper as proclamation—a "sermon" in which the whole congregation participates; the Supper as common worship rather than private devotions; the oneness of the community and the wholeness (health) of the members.

Gifts in Variety and Unity (12:1–31)

The question of the role of spiritual gifts in worship has been raised by the letter from the Corinthians, as the formula "now concerning" indicates (7:1; 8:1). About this matter Paul says, "I do not wish you to remain ignorant" (NEB)—one of his favorite ways to introduce important instruction (10:1; Rom 1:13). Paul begins his instruction by reminding the Corinthians that some of them had experienced religious ecstasy prior to becoming Christians. As heathen, some Corinthians may have been devotees of the Dionysiac cult, a group

especially popular among women, who expressed their faith
by extreme emotional display, including ecstatic speech.
Speaking in tongues is not a distinctive Christian phenomenon; it was practiced in the pagan world and even aroused by
powerless idols.

To ascertain the validity of a religious expression, one
must not rely on emotional feeling, but raise the question: Is it
inspired by the Spirit of God? No one speaking by that spirit,
can say, "Jesus be cursed." Does this mean that within the un-
conscious throes of religious ecstasy someone might even utter an anathema against Jesus? In any case, one thing is clear:
The norm for assessing the authenticity of a Christian experience is the basic confession: "Jesus is Lord" (Rom 10:9; Phil
2:11). A sermon could be developed on the theme: Christ the
Criterion. Of course, it is not enough to say, "Lord, Lord"
(Matt 7:21); authentic confession is not merely mouthing
words, but expressing genuine commitment—acknowledging
the Lordship of Christ in acts of obedience.

Apparently the problem of the church is that some Corinthians suppose there is only one gift of the spirit (speaking in
tongues), and that failure to display that gift is proof of the
spirit's absence. Paul counters this claim with the assertion
that there are "varieties of gifts, but the same Spirit" (v. 4). He
develops this theme by a triad of parallel phrases which express an implicit trinitarian understanding:

varieties of gifts, but the same Spirit;
varieties of service, but the same Lord;
varieties of working, but the same God.

The point of these sayings is that all the functions of the
church—even ordinary kinds of service (*diakonia*)—are ultimately inspired by the one God who manifests himself in different ways. Through his spirit, God imparts gifts to each
believer. These gifts are granted for the common good—for
the building up of the church, rather than the edification of
the individual (14:4). Paul proceeds to list some of the gifts
without intending to be definitive (see Rom 12:6–8).

The emphasis is on the variety of gifts, and on the fact that
the gift which some Corinthians rate highest ("various kinds
of tongues") is low on the list. Along the way, Paul mentions
different types of gifts: gifts of proclamation (the word of wis-

dom and the word of knowledge), gifts of power (faith, heal-
ing, miracle; 2 Cor 12:12; see Rom 15:19), gifts of inspired
speech (prophecy, distinguishing spirits, glossolalia, interpretation). Throughout the list (vv. 8, 9), Paul stresses the point
he makes at the end: "All these are inspired by one and the
same Spirit" (v.11). It is this spirit, the spirit of God, which
distributes the gifts, and the distribution reveals the grace
and freedom of the spirit, rather than the piety of the
recipient.

In v.12, Paul introduces his famous metaphor of the body.
The background from which he borrows the figure is disputed.
It is sometimes traced to the Hebrew concept of corporate per-
sonality or to the hellenistic image of the "Primal Man" in
whose existence all human beings share. According to the Sto-
ics, each individual is a member of one body which comprises
all humanity. Paul's opening statement sounds the theme of
the entire discussion: "For just as the body is one and has
many members, and all the members of the body, though
many, are one body, so it is with Christ."

How do individuals become members of this body?—
through participation in baptism, the initiatory rite (Gal
3:27). And, how are persons sustained in the new life of the
body?—by drinking of the spirit (probably by partaking of the
Lord's Supper; see 10:4). Through these rites, all believers, regardless of ethnic or social origin ("Jews or Greeks, slaves or
free"; see Gal 3:28), are brought into one corporate reality (an
appropriate text for a sermon on unity and diversity—a corporate unity which transcends barriers).

The development of the analogy (vv. 14– 26) makes some
vital points—points which are true for both the metaphor itself (a physical body) and for the object of comparison (the
church). Because one member (a foot or ear) says that it is not
another organ (a hand or eye), that does not make it any less a
part of the body; or, by application, because one person does
not possess the same gift as another, that does not make that
member any less a part of the church. Indeed, a physical body
can function properly only if it is made up of many organs; if
the whole body were eye, it would have no hearing nor sense
of smell. The body is not a single organ; it consists of many
parts, all arranged by God for his purposes. In the same way,
the church is not made up of one sort of person with a particu-

lar gift, but of many people with different gifts—all performing important functions in the economy of God. Moreover, no organ of the body (the eye or the head) can say to another member (the hand or the feet), "I have no need of you." Even the weaker and less presentable parts of the body are indispensable for the healthful functioning of the whole. By "less honorable" and "unpresentable parts," Paul (betraying a puritanical bent) means the sexual organs, which are treated with modesty and honored by being covered with clothing.

The harmonious arrangement of the physical body, according to Paul, has been properly ordered by God the Creator. In applying these illustrations, Paul implies that no member of the community (for example, a tongue speaker) can say he or she has no need of another. Even the weaker members (8:7–13) and those who do not possess the higher gifts (v. 31) are worthy of honor and respect. The ordering of the church—since it is determined by the spirit's gifts—is arranged by God. Instead of asserting spiritual pride which disrupts the church, the members should affirm the depth of God's concern in their care for one another. V. 26 provides a text for a sermon on unity at a depth beneath our perfunctory ecumenical concerns: "If one member suffers, all suffer together; if one member is honored, all rejoice together."

In v. 27, the meaning of the analogy is summarized: "You are the body of Christ, and individually members of it." This indicates that the church is a corporate body, and the individual believers are its functioning members. Some interpreters have claimed that the church is in some real sense Christ's body. This seems to take the body metaphor literally, and to posit an ecclesiology which is too high; it implies an identity between Christ and the church. Although the church is united with Christ, he remains distinct—the Lord of the church. Perhaps the truth which can be preached is this: as body, the church reveals Christ, resembles Christ, and represents Christ (watch the alliteration!). In the context of 1 Cor 12, where attention is focused on gifts performing functions, it may be best to give the body metaphor a functional interpretation: the church can be described as the body of Christ, for in it the work of God begun in him is carried on in the world.

A final paragraph applies the analogy to the order of the church (vv. 27–31). God has appointed leaders and chosen persons to perform important functions (see Rom 12:6–8). Most important are the apostles (persons who have witnessed the resurrection [9:1] and been commissioned to preach [Gal 1:16]), prophets (individuals who proclaim God's message in intelligible speech [14:1–5, 24–25; 1 Thess 5:20]), and teachers (persons who instruct the community in the meaning of God's word [Gal 6:6]).

After mentioning these three kinds of leaders, Paul changes his style and begins again to speak of gifts ("miracles, gifts of healings, helps"; NASB), though he probably intends to emphasize the persons who have received the gifts as the RSV indicates. I've always been glad he included the "administrators"—those mundane types who count the offering and serve on the house and grounds committee. These ordinary folk and their pedestrian tasks are sometimes disparaged by the fancier Christians. Yet, unless the church is built by this kind of unheralded labor, not one brick is put in place! All are not apostles or prophets, and, at the other end of the spectrum, not all can speak in tongues or interpret ecstatic speech. And, even though the gifts are granted by God, Christians should aspire to the higher gifts. Make no mistake about it— not all the gifts are of equal value; one cannot be content with glossolalia if one is able to preach or teach the word with clarity and power.

All Things in Love (13:1–13)

Although one should desire the higher gifts, there is "a still more excellent way"—the way of love. Some commentators believe Paul understands love as the highest of all gifts, but, I think he considers love to be in a category of its own. Love is not a special charisma for a particular believer; love is essential to the existence of every Christian.

Hymns in praise of love and truth are common in hellenistic literature, and the term *agape* is frequently used in the Greek translation of the OT. It is the primary word for God's love in the NT, where it takes on a distinctive meaning. Jesus commanded love for enemies (Matt 5:44; Luke 6:27), and Paul defines love in the light of God's revelation in Christ (see Rom 5:8). This indicates that *agape*, in contrast to other Greek words for love, signifies unmotivated, spontaneous love. The being who loves does not love because the object of love is worth loving, but because it is the nature of that being to love. For this basic Christian theme, the whole chapter can serve as a text, or one can preach on individual themes and various sections of 1 Cor 13.

In the opening section (vv. 1– 3), Paul affirms the superiority of love. First, love is superior to gifts of speech. Suppose one has the gift of glossolalia (12:10, 28, 30), or suppose one can even speak the language of the angels (Hebrew, according to the rabbis!). If the speaker does not have love, he or she becomes a "noisy gong or clanging cymbal"—the sort of instruments which accompanied the ecstatic rites of pagan cults. Second, love is superior to gifts of knowledge and faith. Suppose one has the gift of prophecy (12:10, 28– 29) and is able to perceive the mysteries of God (2:10; 4:1) and understands the hidden *gnosis* (12:8; 8:1), or suppose one has received the power to perform wonders (12:9– 10, 29)—the gift of faith which moves mountains (Mark 11:23); all of this adds up to zero if one does not have *agape*. Love, therefore, is better than theology and more powerful than miracles. Third, love is superior to acts of charity and martyrdom. What if, "I give all my possessions to feed *the poor*" (NASB) or "deliver my body to be burned" as a martyr. Here Paul has stopped preaching to the charismatics and started meddling with us liberals! Isn't contributing our substance to meet the needs of humanity a demonstration of love in action? Isn't suffering self-sacrifice what love is all about? Yet, even good works and martyrdom can be moved by corrupt concerns. If I perform such acts without love, "I gain nothing."

The next part of the chapter (vv. 4– 7) describes the acts of love—shows how love performs the very deeds of charity and self-sacrifice which obedience to God demands. Here love becomes the subject of verbs, and is presented as acting in ways which contradict the conduct of the Corinthians. Love is "patient and kind," while the Corinthians "humiliate those who have nothing" (11:22). Love is not jealous or boastful, arrogant or rude, while the Corinthians are puffed up with pride (5:1; 8:1). And, what is true of the Corinthians is true of Christians in all times; the action of love judges us all. Most of us are irritable and resentful and find it tempting to rejoice in wrong. By way of contrast, "Love keeps no score of wrongs; does not gloat over other men's sins" (NEB). In contrast to our arbitrary action, "Love does not insist on its own way;" love does not function by force, but always works in freedom. Unlike most people, love puts up with everything, believes the best, hopes for the good, endures every trial. "There is nothing love cannot face" (v. 7; NEB). I once heard a sermon in which the preacher invited the hearers to put their names into the text in place of love: "John Doe is patient and kind; John Doe is not jealous or boastful," etc. It doesn't fit, of course, but it should. What love does, we ought to do.

The final section (vv. 8– 13) depicts the endurance of love; "love is eternal" (TEV). The spiritual gifts—tongues, knowledge, and even prophecy—are temporary and will pass away. Glossolalia is not the language of the kingdom; it belongs to the old age which is passing away (7:31). These gifts are temporary because they are incomplete—"imperfect," or "partial" (NEB). Even the knowledge of God which is revealed in Christ (2 Cor 4:6) is not final. And, even the gift of prophecy which edifies the church (14:4) and convicts the unbelievers (14:24) is temporary and incomplete. "When the perfect comes, the imperfect will pass away" (v.10). By "the perfect," Paul no doubt means the eschaton (15:24)—the consummation of God's purposes at the end of history.

In the perspective of this ultimate, the temporary character of the spiritual gifts is illustrated by two analogies, both familiar to hellenistic ears. When one was a child, one acted like a child; when one grows up, one gives up childish ways. The point: spiritual gifts belong to the time not come of age; love belongs to the age of spiritual maturity. "Now we are looking at a dim reflection in a mirror, but then we shall see face to face" (Goodspeed). This illustration was especially vivid for the Corinthians, since their foundries turned out some of the best bronze mirrors of the ancient world. Good as they were, the Corinthian mirrors reflected an imperfect image. Yet, when the end comes, believers shall see God face to face (see Gen 32:20; 2 Cor 3:18). "My knowledge now is partial," continues Paul, "then it will be whole, like God's knowledge of me" (v. 12; NEB). Rather than knowing God, the believer is known by him (Gal 4:9; 1 Cor 8:3); but in the eschaton, the relationship which the priority of God's knowledge has established will be fully realized. "I shall understand fully, even as I have been fully understood."

The text reaches its climax in v. 13: "So faith, hope, love abide, these three; but the greatest of these is love." The expositor who plans a three-point sermon on "things that endure" may wonder at first sight how faith and hope got into the picture at all. Yet, as v. 7 reveals, believing and hoping have already been mentioned as closely related to the action of *agape*. It is also evident that faith and hope endure into the new age, since faith means a continuing dependence on God, and hope looks forward to God's ongoing future. Moreover, the three concepts are basic to Paul's writing, and the triad had already appeared in his earliest letter (1 Thess 1:3; 5:8) in a different order.

In 1 Cor 13, Paul constructs an order of importance where love is last—the greatest. But how is it that love is most important? The answer is that *agape* has its meaning in relation to God. All human loving is tainted by a stain of self interest. *Agape*—spontaneous, self-giving love—is defined by the nature and action of God—the God who "did not spare his own Son" (Rom 8:32). Faith is something *we* do, and hope is something *we* have; love belongs to the being of *God* (see 1 John 4:8, 16).

Speaking with the Mind (14:1–40)

In chap. 14, Paul returns to the question of spiritual gifts. The current popularity of the charismatic movement makes this chapter especially important for preaching and teaching. Whereas the first part of v. 1 mentions love, v. 1b picks up 12:31 ("desire . . . gifts"); the balance of the chapter makes no reference to the "more excellent way" (12:31). Rather than love, the criterion for evaluating gifts has become intelligibility. Consequently, prophecy is to be preferred to speaking in tongues. The latter, as the rest of the chapter shows (vv. 9, 14, 23), describes emotional or ecstatic speech—a common phenomenon in hellenistic religion (see on 12:2 ff). Paul says that "one who speaks in a tongue speaks not to men but to God; for no one understands him" (v. 2). Since God has inspired the speaking, God knows what it means; to ordinary folk what is said remains a mystery. One who prophesies, on the other hand, speaks to people (v. 3). "He who speaks in a tongue edifies himself," says Paul, with an obvious jab at spiritual pride. By way of contrast, "he who prophesies edifies the church."

Paul, therefore, prefers prophecy, and concludes that the one "who prophesies is greater than he who speaks in tongues." Paul is not opposed to speaking in tongues (v. 18, 39); he even recommends it. As a matter of fact, tongues can become virtually the equivalent of prophecy if "someone interprets."

This concern with intelligibility becomes the theme of the next paragraph (vv. 6– 12). Paul recalls his own ministerial endeavor. How could his work benefit a church, he asks, unless it communicated some important instruction: revelation (Gal 1:12), knowledge (2 Cor 4:6), prophecy (Rom 12:6), or teaching (Rom 6:17). He illustrates the point by analogies drawn from music. If flute or harp— instruments used in hellenistic religious ceremonies—do not sound a distinct note, "how can you tell what tune is being played" (v. 7; NEB). "And if the bugle gives an indistinct sound, who will get ready for battle" (a good text for a sermon to preachers; many are playing taps when they ought to sound "charge"!).

The application of the analogies is obvious: "if your ecstatic utterance yields no precise meaning, how can anyone tell what you are saying?" (NEB). To speak without intelligibility is like talking into the air. Paul draws another illustration from linguistics. As the Corinthians who live on the busy isthmus know (see Intro.), there are many languages in the world. If I do not understand a language, however, I am a foreigner (Greek: "barbarian") to the speaker and the speaker is a foreigner to me. This illustration, in which languages are contrasted to tongues, indicates that glossolalia is not a language in the ordinary sense (as some have supposed on the basis of a questionable reading of Acts 2:6– 11); it is a manifestation of the spirit—a gift to be received, not a skill to be acquired. In their zeal for manifestations of the spirit (a note of sarcasm can be detected), the Corinthians ought to be concerned with what is intelligible—the clear and understandable message which builds up the church (a lesson every preacher ought to learn).

The theme of intelligibility is carried on in vv. 13—19. The one who speaks in tongues is urged to pray for the power to interpret. Since interpretation is a gift (12:10), it is something for which one can pray. Here the impression is given that the gift of interpretation is given to the speaker, whereas in 12:30 speaking and interpreting appear to be two different gifts. Paul also indicates (v. 14) that prayer (speech to God; see v. 2) can be expressed by ecstatic speech. In such praying, says Paul, his spirit prays but his mind "contributes nothing" (NAB).

The introduction of the term "mind" provides additional emphasis on the concern for intelligibility. The contrast between mind and spirit suggests a distinction between the mental and emotional or non-rational aspects of one's inner being. Just as prayers ought to involve the rational participation of the worshiper, so singing should be "with the mind" (v. 15). If a blessing or thanksgiving is offered in emotional speech, an outsider (i.e. one who does not understand glossolalia; see v. 23), will not be able to say, "Amen."

As well as showing that liturgical responses were practiced in the early church, this example also makes a point which is relevant today: You cannot participate in worship if you don't know what is going on. To be sure, thanksgiving offered in ecstatic speech is valid for the speaker, but for those who cannot comprehend its meaning, the thanksgiving is not edifying. Paul's next statement (v.18) may come as a surprise to his readers: "I thank God that I speak in tongues more than you all." This comes as a surprise, because Paul rarely practices glossolalia in the church. Paul's experiences of religious ecstasy are private (2 Cor 12:2–4); he is like the individual mentioned in v. 28, "who speaks to himself and to God" (at home). In congregational worship, Paul would rather speak five words with his mind "than ten thousand words in a tongue." For one who can preach and teach the gospel so as "to instruct others," glossolalia is a colossal waste of words.

Next (vv. 20–25), Paul discusses the effect of tongues on non-believers. He opens the discussion with a call to maturity. "Do not be childish, my friends. Be as innocent of evil as babes, but at least be grown-up in your thinking" (NEB). This recalls the analogy of 13:11, and implies that unintelligible speech (glossolalia) is a mark of spiritual immaturity. While Jesus often displays a positive view of children (Mark 10:15; Matt 18:3; Luke 18:17), Paul frequently uses children as negative illustrations (3:1–2). Perhaps the difference (for one seeking a homiletical theme) is the distinction between being child*like* and child*ish*. Paul advances his argument by a citation from the OT (Isa 28:11). According to Paul, this text means that when God speaks to people through a foreign language, they do not understand. In the same way, people will not be able to comprehend a message delivered through glossolalia. Paul's exegetical statement, however, is somewhat confusing: "Thus, tongues are a sign not for believers" (v. 22). What he means, as the following verses make clear, is that tongues are a sign that the message is not understood—a sign of unbelief. Prophecy, on the other hand, is a sign which can be understood—a sign which leads to belief.

Paul's interpretation is illustrated by a description of Corinthian worship. If everyone speaks in tongues, outsiders or unbelievers will say that the worshipers are mad. If, on the other hand, all the members of the congregation prophecy (though in turn and in order; v. 31), then unbelievers or outsiders will hear the message of the church, be convicted, called to account, see themselves as they really are, and fall down and worship God. Whereas no attempt is being made to present a formal analysis of conversion, some of the constituent elements are implied: hearing, repentance, confession, faith (Rom 10:9– 10; 1 Thess 1:9). It is also apparent that the primary function of early Christian prophecy is not to predict the future, but to proclaim the word—the word through which God is active in the church (v. 25) and to which the hearer can respond (Rom 10:17). For evangelism, we can conclude, speaking in tongues is counter-productive.

In vv. 26– 36, Paul makes a final plea for good order. His picture of the worshipping congegation provides a glimpse of the early church at worship. The service apparently contained a mixture of spontaneous flexibility and traditional formality inherited from the synagogue. Congregational participation is suggested by the words, "each of you contributes a hymn, some instruction, a revelation, an ecstatic utterance, or the interpretation of such an utterance" (NEB). As to glossolalia, no more than two or three speakers are to be allowed, and each must speak in turn. If there is no one to interpret, speaking in tongues is not to be permitted in public worship; it is a private matter between the speaker and God (see v. 19). These requirements indicate that glossolalia does not represent an uncontrollable ecstatic experience; the speaker retains responsibility. Similar restrictions are placed on prophets. Even this more important gift should be practiced by only two

or three persons per service. And if, in the middle of prophesy-
ing, revelation is granted to another prophet, the first must be
quiet. Prophecy, too, is to be done in turn, so that the congregation can hear and understand. Other prophets evaluate
what is being said, for "the spirits of the prophets are subject
to prophets." This prophetic consensus is responsible to the
ultimate norm—the God who is the source of all inspiration
who is "not a God of confusion, but of peace" (v. 33).

Paul's conclusion about orderliness includes his notori-
ous dictum that "women should keep silence in the churches"
(v. 34). Although interpolation theories should not be quickly
embraced, the case against the authenticity of vv. 34–36 is
strong. For one thing, this material is located in a different
place in some manuscripts, and the text includes some
phrases not typical of Paul. The demand of silence is contra-
dicted by Paul's advice that women should pray and prophesy
with a veil (11:5,13), and inconsistent with his basic affirmation in Gal 3:28. If the text is authentic, it may indicate that
Paul is facing a particular problem in Corinth. Many of those
abusing the gifts of tongues could have been women (see on
12:1–31). The notion that women should be subordinate, of
course, is in harmony with 11:2–16, and the text Paul has in
mind could have been Gen 3:16. The view that women should
maintain a low profile in public and be in submission to their
husbands was shared by Paul's contemporaries and emphasized later by the Pauline School (Eph 5:22; Col 3:18; 1 Tim
2:11–12). As chap. 11 suggests, Paul does not believe the
church's primary function is to serve as innovator of cultural
styles; the word of God did not originate with the avant-garde
of Corinth. Nevertheless, Paul's recognition of the importance
of feminine leadership in the church is attested by his praise
of Phoebe, Prisca, and other women in Rom 16.

The final word on the spiritual gifts is stated in vv. 37–
40. Here Paul mentions, along with the prophet, the "spiritual
person" (Barrett)— a category which probably includes other
ecstatics as well as the speakers in tongues. When he claims
that his instruction is "a command of the Lord," Paul does not
appear to have in mind a citation from the historical Jesus (as
in 7:10). More likely, he is expressing his conviction that his
teaching in general has apostolic authority. This interpretation is confirmed by his conclusion that one who does not rec-

ognize this authority will not be recognized (see 14:38 and 11:16). The final verses echo the theme of 14:1. As Paul has said elsewhere in the chapter (vv. 5, 18), speaking in tongues is to be permitted though prophecy is preferred. The criterion then and now is the intelligible message of the gospel which promotes good order in the church.

The Resurrection of the Dead
(1 Corinthians 15:1 – 58)

Chap. 15 treats an issue of ultimate importance. Our preaching should return to this issue again and again, always grounded on solid exegesis. Paul considers the question because it is a problem at Corinth (see v. 12). He begins the discussion by asserting that witness to the resurrection is essential to preaching the gospel. In a way which suggests a sermon outline, Paul declares that the gospel (see on 1:17) is basic for Christian existence: it is the gospel "which you received" (by a decision of the past), "in which you stand" (in your present life-style), "by which you are saved" (looking to the future).

In his preaching, Paul delivers what he received, and the words translated "delivered" and "received" are technical terms for the transmitting of tradition. This tradition can be reduced to a few basic elements—the things "of first importance." Sometimes described as the *kerygma*, these basic elements constitute a summary of the proclamation of the early church. At base, there are two:

Christ died and was buried;
Christ was raised and appeared.

The burial confirms the death, and the appearances are the means by which the resurrection is perceived. The idea that Christ died "for our sins" (Rom 5:8; 2 Cor 5:14) means that the saving power of God's love is disclosed in the sacrifice of his own son (Rom 8:32). Like most of the NT, Paul expresses the conviction that Christ *was raised* (passive); "God raised him from the dead" (Rom 10:9). Exactly what Scriptures Paul has in mind is difficult to determine. For Christ's death for sins, he may be thinking of Isa 53:5; and for the resurrection on the third day, he may be alluding to texts like Ps 16:10 and Hos 6:2. Perhaps the phrase "in accordance with the Scriptures" is primarily a way to affirm that the events of death and resurrection are according to the will of God.

The list of resurrection appearances is probably part of the tradition which Paul received. To this tradition, Paul appears to add material of his own, especially his comment about the five hundred (v. 6b), and his report of his own experience (v. 8). It is evident from the Greek construction (then . . . then . . . then) that the list of appearances is to be understood as representing chronological order. According to this order, Cephas (the Aramaic word for "Peter") was the first to whom the risen Christ appeared (in contrast to Matt 28:9– 10, but confirmed by Like 24:34). "The twelve" designates a stereotyped group of leading disciples, since the appearance would have been only to the eleven (Matt 28:16 ff). For the appearance to "five hundred brethren" no other text can be found, though attempts have been made to relate their experience to the events of Pentecost (Acts 2:1– 42). The appearance to this large group "at one time" shows that the event was not a private hallucinatory experience, but a public happening which could be verified by those who "are still alive." The appearance to James (the brother of Jesus) could have been confirmed during Paul's visit to Jerusalem three years after his conversion (Gal 1:18– 19). Who is included in "all the apostles" cannot be ascertained, though Paul probably conceives of a group larger than the twelve. For Paul, a resurrection appearance is prerequisite for apostleship (9:1).

Most interesting is the appearance to Paul (v. 8). Here we have the account of a resurrection appearance by an eyewitness. It is clear that Paul understands the appearance to himself to be no different from the rest. To be sure, he does say that he was "untimely born," but the term actually describes an abortion or miscarriage. This term probably refers to what follows rather than to what precedes—to the confession that Paul is "least of the apostles" and "unfit to be called an apostle" (v. 9). Thus, his birth into Christianity was premature and violent (NEB: "monstrous"), that is, traumatic and without the benefit of the preparation which others had enjoyed. When he says that the appearance to him was "last of all," Paul indicates that he knows of no others which occurred during the twenty years which have elapsed since his own experience. This, in my judgment, makes an important theological point: resurrection appearances do not continue indefinitely: they belong to the total revelatory event which occurs within the limits of history—the event of the life, death, and resurrection (appearances) of Christ.

The problem of the next paragraph is to determine what is being denied when some say "there is no resurrection of the dead" (v. 12). Older interpreters thought this reflected hellenistic skepticism about life after death, or that it represented a Greek belief in immortality of the soul in contrast to the Jewish-Christian concept of resurrection (see on vv. 53–54). More recently, it has become popular to believe that the Corinthians are denying the reality of the future resurrection. While they acknowledge the resurrection of Christ (as v. 12a assumes), they imagine that the resurrection of Christians has *already* been realized in the spiritual experience of the believer (4:8; see 2 Tim 2:18).

In any case, Paul is convinced that the resurrection of Christ assures the resurrection of Christians at the end of history. In a first line of argument (v.13), he says that if there is no resurrection at all, then Christ has not been raised. If Christ has not been raised, Paul's preaching is in vain and the response to that preaching—the Corinthians' faith—is also in vain. The lesson for preachers is clear: Witness to the resurrection of Christ is basic to the Christian proclamation.

In a second line of argument (v.16), Paul proceeds to draw the implications of the denial of Christ's resurrection for Christian existence. If Christ has not been raised, faith in him is futile, and those who believe are still trapped in their sins. This means that those who have died in Christ are no different from the non-believers; they are not being saved, but are perishing (2 Cor 2:15). The resurrection, therefore, is crucial for faith, not in the sense that it guarantees immortality, but in the fact that it declares the event of the crucified Christ to be the redemptive action of God (Rom 1:4). The believer can face the uncertain future with confidence. "If it is for this life only that Christ has given us hope, we of all men are most to be pitied" (v.19; NEB). Vv. 17–19 suggest a sermon on the theme: "The Meaning of the Resurrection"—for faith, for ethics (sin), for hope.

In the next paragraph (vv.20–28), Paul describes the events of the end—events which include the future resurrection which the Corinthians deny. He begins with imagery borrowed from the OT: the resurrection of Christ is like the

offering of the first fruits of the harvest (Lev 23:10– 11)–an
offering which stands for the whole crop. The oneness of
Christ with the new humanity is illustrated by the analogy of
Adam and Christ (see v. 45). This analogy indicates that the
old humanity (all who are in Adam) are subject to death (Rom
5:12); the new humanity (all who have faith in Christ) are destined for life (1 Thess 5:9). The future resurrection, however,
will fit into an order of events. These events have started to
unfold with the resurrection of Christ, so that the long-
awaited age of the messiah has already dawned. At the future
coming of Christ–the parousia or triumphant return of the
risen Lord–those who belong to Christ will also be raised (1
Thess 4:15– 16). Then comes the end of history when Christ
delivers the kingdom to God.

Taking up the apocalyptic theme of a final battle with the
forces of evil, Paul declares that Christ will destroy every rule,
power, and authority (Rom 8:38)–a victory which fulfills the
expectation of Ps 110:1. The fact that death is singled out as
the last (or ultimate) enemy anticipates vv. 54– 57, and indicates that Paul understands the evil forces in existential
terms. The real issue is not the dethroning of demonic powers,
but the overcoming of death–the evil which threatens human
existence. Although Ps 8:6 predicts the subjection of all things
to God, there is an exception, namely, the one who subjects all
things to God, that is, Christ. Finally, Christ himself will be
subjected to God (3:23) so that "God may be all in all"
(NASB); God's ultimate purposes will finally be achieved
(Rom 11:36).

Vv. 29– 34 present additional arguments to support belief in the future resurrection. First, Paul mentions people who
are "being baptized on behalf of the dead." Nobody knows for
sure what this means. Perhaps Paul is referring to vicarious
baptism whereby one was able to stand in for a person who
had died without participating in the ritual. For such a rite to
have any significance, argues Paul, the reality of the resurrection would have to be assumed. Paul also argues that the resurrection faith makes it possible to endure a life like his own,
fraught with dangers (2 Cor 11:26). The reference to "beasts at
Ephesus" is probably not to an actual encounter in the arena,
but is a figurative way to describe the serious threats Paul
continually faces (2 Cor 1:8).

If there is no resurrection, one might just as well eat and drink—live as though this life is all there is. Rather than conforming to the values of this world (Rom 12:2), Christian existence ought to be determined by the ultimate (an obvious sermonic theme). Paul supports his argument by a quotation from Menander: "Bad company corrupts good morals" (NASB). If you run around with people who live by the trivial, your life will be corrupted, too. To hope in the resurrection, on the other hand, is to set life in its eternal framework. Therefore, "come back to a sober and upright life and leave your sinful ways" (v. 34; NEB). Failure to do so represents ignorance of God.

In an effort to discredit Paul's argument, his opponents ask, "How are the dead raised? With what kind of body do they come?" (v. 35). Their criticism assumes that a future resurrection would entail a resuscitation of the corpse. Such a literal notion of the resurrection was entertained by some rabbis who liked to debate whether the body would be raised naked or clothed. To these questions, Paul retorts, You foolish person! Borrowing an analogy from botany, he says that a seed will not come to life unless it dies, and that the plant which it becomes is different from the seed. Who, looking at a dried-up bulb, would imagine that it could produce an Easter lily? There are all sorts of bodies—animals, birds, fish, says Paul. There are earthly and heavenly bodies, and the various celestial bodies—sun, moon, stars—differ in radiance. In vv. 42–44, Paul applies the analogy: "So it is with the resurrection of the dead." Here, too, the emphasis is on contrast:

sown perishable, raised imperishable;
sown in dishonor, raised in power;
sown a physical body, raised a spiritual body.

The contrasts make it evident that the resurrection body is not to be construed in terms of the earthly.

Precisely what Paul means by the "spiritual body" is a matter of vigorous debate. The word translated body (soma) can stand for the whole person, so that Paul may be referring to a reality which is personal in character. Or, he may be suggesting that the new body is composed of spirit, or that the new reality, though spiritual, has a definite (bodily) character. In any case, Paul's rudimentary meaning is clear: the resurrection reality is different from the physical body. Picking up the Adam-Christ analogy again (v. 22), Paul argues that there are two humanities. The first man (Adam) became a living soul (Gen 2:7); the second man (Christ) became a life-giving spirit. The first is earthly, made of dust; the second is heavenly, spiritual in nature. All people bear the image of the old humanity with an earthly body destined for death; believers will bear the image of the heavenly man with hope of being raised from the dead. Although Paul advocates a "spiritual resurrection," he does not understand it as some imaginary or nebulous phenomenon. The spiritual body is a body—a new reality.

In the final analysis, the events of the end remain a mystery (v. 51). Not all shall sleep, says Paul, meaning that not all people will die before the end comes. All, including both those who will die and those who expect to be alive (including Paul), will be transformed into the likeness of Christ's glorious body (Phil 3:21). The change will occur suddenly, in an instant ("in a twinkling of an eye"), at the sound of the eschatological trumpet (Matt 24:31; 1 Thess 4:16). Two sorts of transformation will take place: the dead shall be raised imperishable (the perishable nature shall put on imperishable), and the living be changed (the mortal shall put on immortality). The metaphor of putting on is reminiscent of the hellenistic symbol of being clothed with a heavenly garment (2 Cor 5:4).

In preaching, I believe the term "immortality" should be used with caution. Paul does not ascribe to the Greek notion that everyone is endowed with an eternal spirit which is released from the body at death. Instead, he believes that the whole person dies (body and spirit), and that resurrection is a new creative act of God.

Let the preacher take note: life after death is not a human attribute, but a gift of God's grace. After the transformation of the dead and the living, the prediction of the OT will be fulfilled. A combination of Isa 25:8 and Hos 13:14 is cited to declare that "death is swallowed up in victory," and the "sting of death" is overcome. The sting of death, according to Paul, is sin, because death is the penalty for sin (Gen 2:17; Rom 5:12). The victory over sin is accomplished by Christ through whom God works to free us from sin and death. Thus, the believer can say, "Thanks be to God" (Rom 7:25). This affirmation becomes the motivation for moral endeavor (a sermonic theme). Confident in the ultimate victory, the Christian can "be steadfast, immovable, always abounding in the work of the Lord." The conviction that this "labor is not in vain" does not posit salvation by works, it affirms that those who look to the ultimate participate in the fulfillment of the purposes of God.

The Offering, Travel Plans, and Greetings
(1 Corinthians 16:1–24)

At the Jerusalem conference, Paul had agreed to take up an offering in his churches for the poor Christians of the holy city (Gal 2:10). The reference to "the churches of Galatia" indicates that Paul has pursued this task over a broad geographical area (see Rom 15:25–28). Collecting the offering constituted a continuing problem, as 2 Cor 8 and 9 indicate. Apparently the method of collection was for each member to save an amount of money on a weekly basis. Though the "first day" of the week is probably the time of worship, the collection seems to have been handled as an individual responsibility. A Christian's giving, as a budget sermon could emphasize, is free and proportional—"in proportion to what he has earned" (v. 2; TEV). When Paul comes to Corinth, he does not want to have to function as a fund raiser. However, he is prepared to send the accredited delegates of the Corinthian church to Jerusalem with the offering, and, if it proves advisable, to accompany them himself. As it turned out, Paul did decide to take the collection to Jerusalem (Rom 15:25), thereby expressing a commitment to a benevolent offering which finally cost him imprisonment and death.

Next, the apostle relates his travel plans and the travel plans of his associates. Paul intends to go through Macedonia on his way to Corinth—an itinerary which was later followed (2 Cor 2:13; 7:5). He expects simply to pass through Macedonia (probably visiting the churches at Philippi and Thessalonica), but hopes to stay some time in Corinth, perhaps to spend the winter there. In any case, Paul's plans must conform to the will of God (see Rom 1:10). For the time being, he will stay in Ephesus, "for a wide door of effective work" (v. 9) has opened. Like every alert minister, Paul is sensitive to opportunities to advance the gospel, and the metaphor of the door, which he uses elsewhere (2 Cor 2:12), provides a text for a sermon on evangelism. Church work always encounters adversaries, and for Paul, this means "fighting with beasts" (15:32) and suffering affliction (2 Cor 1:8). Timothy has already been sent (4:17), and when he arrives, he should be given no "cause to be afraid" (v. 10; NASB). Apparently, some members of the Pauline churches were inclined to denigrate the work of his assistants. Paul (in contrast to some "senior" ministers) supported his associates with confidence: Timothy is doing the "work of the Lord" as surely as Paul is (see 1 Thess 3:2). Paul had also hoped that Apollos (1:12; 4:6) might visit the church, too, but that was not now in accord with God's will (or Apollos'; the Greek is not clear).

Typical of the Pauline letters, the conclusion includes advice and admonition (vv. 13 – 18). The Corinthians are urged to "be watchful" (1 Thess 5:6) and to "stand firm" in their faith (15:1, 58; Gal 5:1). In this time of trial when the end is at hand, Christians are encouraged to "act like men" (NAB) — a hellenistic admonition to courage which has possibilities for preaching. Paul's summary of the kind of conduct which should characterize Christian living provides a text for a sermon: "Let all that you do be done in love" (v. 14; see chap. 13). As Paul had instructed the Thessalonians (1 Thess 5:12 – 13), the Corinthians should respect their leaders. Paul mentions especially the household of Stephanas (whose baptism he had almost forgotten! 1:16). People of this sort should be respected because they have devoted themselves to the ministry (diakonia) of the "saints," that is, their fellow-Christians. This advice suggests a sermon on responsibility to the church's leadership, whereby it could be shown that inordinate loyalty to leaders leads to factionalism (1:12 – 13), while appropriate regard for leaders promotes unity and the upbuilding of the church. Stephanas, Fortunatus and Achaicus have come to visit Paul, perhaps bringing the letter from the church (7:1).

Finally, Paul conveys the greetings of the churches of the province of Asia (v. 19) and urges the Christians to greet one another "with a holy kiss" — the Christian adaptation of the customary hellenistic embrace (1 Thess 5:26; Rom 16:16; 2 Cor 13:12).

The way Paul addresses this advice to the congregation suggests that his letter is to be read as a part of the Corinthian worship service. This is also implied by his use of the liturgical formula: *Marana tha*—Aramaic words which probably mean, "Our Lord, come!" Since the earliest days of the Palestinian church, Christians have been pronouncing this petition in their services of worship. By it, they are invoking the presence of the risen Christ into their worship, and expecting his triumphant return (15:23; 1 Thess 4:15). I believe today's worship could use some of their vitality, and a sermon on *marana tha*—the presence and future of the Lord—might contribute to that end.

The conclusion of the letter includes Paul's personal greeting, written in the large letters of his own hand (Gal 6:11; Phlm 19). Paul also sounds a discordant note: one who does not love the Lord should be accursed (see Gal 1:8–9). The word for love here is *phileo* (its only use in Paul); the text makes the important point that the other side of love (the rejection of love) is judgment. The letter ends with a two-fold benediction:

> The grace of the Lord Jesus be with you.
> My love be with you all in Christ Jesus.

2 CORINTHIANS

Address and Blessing
(2 Corinthians 1:1–11)

Written from Macedonia around AD 56, 2 Cor 1–9 can be characterized as the "letter of reconciliation" (see Intro.). The troubles which led to Paul's hurried trip from Ephesus to Corinth, and which provoked his severe letter (2 Cor 10–13) have been resolved. Written in a mood of thanksgiving, the letter constitutes an expression in praise of ministry and serves as an inspiration for preachers in every generation. The letter, like 1 Corinthians, begins with the usual formalities. Paul is joined in the address by Timothy who is described as "our brother" (i.e. a fellow-Christian). Timothy had participated in the original mission to Corinth (Acts 18:5), and is apparently with Paul at the time of writing.

The thanksgiving paragraph which is conventional in the Pauline letters is replaced by a benediction (vv. 3–11). Instead of saying, "I give thanks" (1 Cor 1:4), Paul writes, "Blessed be the God and Father of our Lord Jesus Christ" (see Eph 1:3; 1 Pet 1:3). The expression is typical of Judaism (see Ps 72:18), and Jewish liturgical features are reflected throughout the blessing. Perhaps Paul uses a benediction here because he is offering praise to God for his own deliverance, whereas in other letters he is expressing thanks to God for the church. A sermon on the doctrine of God may be suggested by the portrayal of the Almighty as the "Father of all mercies" and the

"God of all comfort" (OT concepts; see Isa 51:12). The theme
of comfort in affliction dominates the paragraph. The basis of
comfort is the God who comforts the afflicted. Comforted by
him, they in turn become the ministers of the comforting mercy of God. This God is the Father of Jesus Christ whose sufferings the apostle shares (see Phil 3:10). If Paul is afflicted, it is
for the salvation of his churches (see 4:12); if he is comforted,
it is for their comfort. Though all Christians will not endure
the same sort of sufferings as Paul (11:23 ff), they will surely
experience the trials which accompany the crises of the
world's demise (1 Cor 7:26). We Christians, who enjoy the
creature comforts, need to be reminded that suffering belongs
to the essence of Christianity (Rom 5:3), that in the center of
our faith stands a cross. To share Christ's sufferings, however,
is to share his comforting presence and love, for the Christian
hope is secure (see v. 9).

The exact nature of Paul's affliction in Asia (v. 8) cannot
be determined. No doubt he refers to something which has
transpired since he wrote 1 Corinthians. Although any of the
trials listed in 2 Cor 11:23 is a possibility, I believe Paul may
be describing an imprisonment. This seems suggested by his
reference to a "sentence of death"—a verdict which Paul had
psychologically accepted. Since he had abandoned hope in
himself, Paul had been forced to rely on the ultimate ground
of hope, "God who raises the dead" (see Rom 4:17). There is a
sermon here on hope when life has become hopeless—hope in
the God of the future whose faithfulness has been confirmed
by the raising of Christ. Paul's hope was not ill-founded, for
God had delivered him from the "deadly peril" (v. 10), and he
would do it again; dangers never end. In other thanksgiving
paragraphs, Paul expresses his prayers for the Christians
(Rom 1:9–10, 1 Thess 1:2–3), but here he requests the
prayers of the Corinthians on his own behalf. This text also
teaches us that ministers need prayer, too; the ministry is supported by the prayers of the church.

Changed Plans and Faithful Purposes

(2 Corinthians 1:12–2:13)

Paul not only requests prayer for deliverance from trouble in Asia, he also covets understanding in regard to his relations with Corinth. In particular, he wants the Corinthians to recognize that his changes in travel plans do not warrant a charge of vacillation. Paul's boast, in the face of such charges, is that his conduct is above reproach. To this, his conscience bears witness, acquitting him of wrongdoing (see Rom 2:15). His behavior, especially toward the Corinthians (see 1 Cor 9:15), has been marked by "holiness" and "sincerity." Paul's conduct has not been moved by "fleshly wisdom"(NASB; see 1 Cor 1:20; 2:6; 3:19), but "by the grace of God."

Like his missionary itinerary, Paul's letters reflect the same sort of integrity. He writes plainly, without attempt to deceive. As a matter of fact, Paul had written a set of travel plans in 1 Cor 16:5–9, and later changed these plans, and then failed to follow through with the changes (see vv. 15–16). No wonder he hopes the Corinthians will be understanding! Although understanding is only partial now, it will be full when the final purposes of ministry are manifest. Then—on the day of the Lord (1 Cor 1:8; 5:5)—the Corinthians will be able to be proud of Paul (5:12) as he already is proud of them (7:4). In the final recounting, faithful preachers will be able to be proud of their work (1 Cor 9:1; 3:16; 1 Thess 2:19).

The revising of travel plans is explained in vv. 15–17. Rather than coming to Corinth via Macedonia (1 Cor 16:5–9), Paul had decided to visit the Corinthians before and after his trip to Macedonia ("a double visit"; NEB). The Corinthians had probably learned of this new proposal from Paul himself during the "painful visit" (see Intro.). His failure to follow the plan was evident in the fact that he had not come to Corinth, but had traveled to Macedonia first (2:13; 7:5). Although the Corinthians were no doubt concerned with Paul's failure to come, he gives primary attention to his intentions. He does not make plans according to his own whims ("according to the flesh"; NASB). Paul's word is responsible to God and "is not an ambiguous blend of Yes and No" (v. 18; NEB). These words, along with Matt 5:37 and Jas 5:12, provide texts for a sermon on personal integrity. Paul formulates his words so as to be in harmony with the larger word, the word of preaching. The word which Silvanus, Timothy and Paul preached when they first came to town (Acts 18:5) was Jesus Christ, the Son of God, God's great affirmation. This potent sermonic theme finds its text in v. 20: "All the promises of God find their Yes in him." For me, the important point is not what particular promises Paul has in mind, but the fact that Christ is affirmed to be the fulfillment of God's redemptive purposes (Rom 9:5; 11:26; Gal 3:16). The promises of God are defined in the light of Jesus Christ. Just as God says "Yes" in Christ, so the preacher and the hearer can utter an affirmation of their own, "Amen!"(1 Cor 14:16).

God's Yes in Christ affirms his promises for preacher and hearer alike. Paul develops this theme in vv. 21–22, and provides an interesting sermon outline. Four images are used: (1) God "establishes us." The word translated "establish" can be used as a commercial or legal term to refer to a guaranteed security or valid will. In Christ, God writes a receipt which assures his concern for the believer's life. (2) God has "anointed us" (NASB). The use of the word *chrisas* (anointed) is a wordplay on *Christos;* it is used only here in Paul. In the OT, priests and kings are anointed by God to do his work (see 1 Pet 2:9). (3) God "has put his seal upon us." A seal of wax bears the impression of the one who seals, and authorizes the document which it seals. In Christ, God has put his imprint upon us (see 1 Cor 9:2) so that we will "bear the image of the man of heaven" (1 Cor 15:49). (4) God has "given us his Spirit" as a "pledge" (JB; NEB). The word translated "pledge" (RSV: "guarantee") stands for a first installment which gives assurance that the rest of the payment will come. The gift of the spirit is God's down payment on the promise of life in the coming age. Taken together, these four images show how the life of the believer is totally dependent on the grace of God.

In v. 23, Paul presents his reason for failing to follow his travel plans—a reason whose validity is witnessed by God

(Rom 1:9; Phil 1:8, 1 Thess 2:5; contrast Matt 5:34–36). Paul refrained from visiting the Corinthians in order to spare them pain. Because of this kind of concern, Paul had made up his mind not to make "another painful visit" (2:1). These words indicate that an earlier painful visit had in fact been made (see Intro.). Though that visit had caused the Corinthians sorrow, they are the very ones who can make him glad—by their repentance. Paul's severe letter was designed to bring about penitent sorrow, for he had written "out of much affliction and anguish of heart and with many tears" (v. 4). Although the letter had made them sorry (7:8), its ultimate intent was to present Paul's chastening love.

In v. 5, Paul begins some cryptic remarks about a particular offender. This offender cannot be identified with the incestuous man of 1 Cor 5, since too much time and too many events have intervened. Besides, this latter offender has primarily attacked Paul, though he has indirectly injured the church. He probably had attacked the apostle during the "painful visit," and may have been a leader of the opposition which questioned Paul's apostleship (2 Cor 10–13). In any case, this offender has been dealt a serious punishment by the majority of the congregation. Repentance has apparently resulted, for Paul recommends forgiveness, comfort and reaffirmation of love. Excessive sorrow could overwhelm the offender, and failure to forgive can play into the hands of Satan, the tempter (1 Cor 7:5). There is an important sermonic truth here: zeal for righteous judgment can become captive to the demonic.

All these troubles with Corinth have distressed the apostle. He had left Ephesus and moved on to Troas in the hope of meeting Titus. This fellow-worker had probably been the bearer of the severe letter, and his return to Paul would bring news of its effect upon the Corinthians. Although a door of evangelistic opportunity had been opened in Troas, Paul decided to abandon that work because of his anxiety about Corinth. Instructive in a negative fashion is the fact that pastoral problems in a contentious church can derail the primary mission of the ministry. In order to meet Titus and acquire news of the situation at Corinth, Paul travels to Macedonia.

Triumph and Trials in Ministry
(2 Corinthians 2:14–7:4)

Sufficiency for Ministry (2:14–3:6)

Assuming the unity of 2 Cor 1-9 (see Intro.), we note that Paul has interrupted the discussion of his travel itinerary to present an excursus on the ministry. The mention of Macedonia recalls the good news which Paul had learned there (7:5–7), and inspires him to write a composition on the wonders of the ministerial task. This section of 2 Corinthians presents one of the most moving portrayals of ministry to be found anywhere in Scripture. I find in it abundant texts for sermons directed not only to the professionals, but to all believers who take their Christian vocation seriously.

The passage begins with the vivid figure of the triumphal procession. After an important military triumph, victorious generals paraded through Rome, hailed as conquerors and displaying their defeated foes. "Thanks be to God" (see 1 Cor 15:57), exclaims Paul, "who always leads us in triumph." While he is no doubt using the figure, Paul's conception of the application of the imagery is not entirely clear. Are the ministers viewed as "captives in Christ's triumphal procession" (NEB) or "partners of his triumph" (JB)? In light of Paul's paradoxical perception of ministry (1 Cor 15:9–10), he may imply both. The minister is at the same time captive of Christ (10:5) and fellow-conqueror with him (Rom 8:37).

The mention of "fragrance" (NASB: "sweet aroma") is probably suggested by incense which was burned during triumphal processions, but in Paul's facile mind another image appears: the sweet savor of sacrifices wafting upward to God (Gen 8:21; Exod 29:18; Lev 1:9). The minister who is captive of Christ is also sacrifice (see 4:11; Phil 2:17). Through this sacrificial ministry, the knowledge of God is revealed (4:6)—a challenging duty for the preacher. This ministry, like the word of the cross (1 Cor 1:18), has a paradoxical effect: to those "who are being saved," it is a "fragrance from life to life"; for those who are perishing, it is "a deadly stench that kills" (TEV). The process of salvation and judgment has already begun with the response to the ministry of the gospel, for in it both righteousness and wrath are revealed (Rom 1:17– 18). Faced with this ministerial responsibility, Paul cries out, "Who is sufficient for these things?" (v. 16). An answer will be offered in 3:5, but for the time being, one thing is clear: peddlers of God's message—those who engage in ministry for personal gain— are not sufficient. The imagery of this passage provides sermonic possibilities: minister as captive and conqueror, ministry as sacrifice, paradox of ministry, peddlers and prophets.

Since Paul has implied high claims for his ministry, a question can be raised, "Are we beginning to commend ourselves again?" (3:1). The issue of commendation is thematic to this part of the epistle (4:2; 5:12; 6:4). Paul's opponents, who have made the accusation, had apparently tried to authorize their own work by carrying letters of recommendation. The epistle of recommendation—a formal letter-type in the hellenistic world—was carried by a person who was commended to the recipient of the letter by the letter's writer (see Rom 16:1). Paul insists that he does not need such letters, for, "You yourselves are our letter of recommendation" (v. 2; a text for a sermon). What commends Paul is the fruit of his labor, manifest in a faithful church (see 1 Cor 9:1). Paul and his colleagues carry this "letter" written on their hearts (RSV margin; see 7:3). The letter is read by all who observe their work, and its author—the ultimate source of Paul's commendation—is Christ. Unlike an ordinary letter written with ink, this epistle is inscribed by the spirit of God (see Exod 31:18). The allusion to God's writing suggests another metaphor: the new convenant, written not on stone but on human hearts (Jer 31:33). The claim that Paul is minister of the new covenant raises again the question of sufficiency (v. 16). In answer, Paul confesses that he is not sufficient on his own (1 Cor 15:9); his sufficiency is from God. The new covenant is not a legal agreement, inscribed on stone; but a personal relationship, written on the hearts of people. Sermons could be preached on "God's sufficiency," or on the ministry of the new covenant, a ministry of the spirit which gives life.

Fading Splendor and Ministry of Glory (3:7– 18)

The idea of being a minister of the new covenant leads Paul into a comparison between the new ministry and the old, the ministry of Moses. The thematic word is *diakonia* (ministry or service) which the RSV mistranslates "dispensation." Throughout the passage, Paul employs a rabbinic method of interpretation. According to Exod 34:29– 34, the face of Moses, after he had talked with God, shone with a radiance which terrified the people. Moses, therefore, put on a veil when he spoke with the people and removed the veil when he conversed with God.

In exegeting the text, Paul acknowledges that the ministry of Moses was a ministry of glory (RSV: "splendor")—a glory symbolized by the radiant face of Moses. The glory of that ministry is inferior, however, since it was the ministry of the convenant of the letter which kills (v. 6). Thus it was a ministry of condemnation and death, in contrast to the ministry of the spirit which reveals righteousness (Rom 1:17) and offers life. Moreover, the glory of Moses' ministry was fading and temporary, so that it is inferior to the glory of the new ministry which abides.

In making this point, Paul attributes an ulterior motive to Moses: the reason he put the veil on his face was to prevent the people from seeing "the end of the fading splendor" (v. 13). Although Paul might have derived this interpretation from the evidence that Moses appears later in the Exodus narrative without a veil, the notion that Moses engaged in deception of the Israelites would seem to most Jewish exegetes to be little short of blasphemy. Actually, some rabbis believed that the face of Moses continued to reflect the divine glory until his death. Making further use of the allegory of the veil, Paul asserts that the veil which was on the face of Moses is now on the minds of the Jews. Whenever the OT is read, a veil lies over the minds (literally, "hearts") of the hearers, so that they are unable to understand what the scriptures mean (see Rom 11:7– 8). The veil can only be removed by Christ; he is the true revelation of the meaning of the OT (see Rom 10:5– 13). This suggests a sermon on Christ the revealer who unveils the truth of God. Paul bases this concept on his interpretation of Exod 34:34: When Moses turned to speak with the Lord (God), he took off the veil; when believers turn to the Lord (Christ), the veil is taken away. The risen Lord can be identified with the spirit (Rom 8:9– 11), for he is the one who ratifies the new covenant (1 Cor 11:25) of the spirit (v. 6). Where the spirit of Christ is "there is freedom" (a sermonic text)—freedom to turn to the Lord, to remove the veil, to perceive God's revelation (see Rom 8:2).

V. 18 provides a text for a sermon on "the transforming vision." In the hellenistic world, a vision of a deity could change the beholder into a new being. Paul's expression of this concept is ambiguous. The translation may read: "we all reflect as in a mirror the splendour of the Lord" (NEB); or: "we all, with unveiled face, beholding the glory of the Lord." The former would focus on Moses who reflected the glory of God— a possibility for people created in the image of God (Gen 1:27) whose hearts reflect the light of God's glory (4:4). The latter translation would contrast those who behold with those who arc veiled and unable to see the divine glory (vv. 14– 15). In either case, to reflect or to behold the glory of the Lord is to be transformed. It is to anticipate the appropriation of the image of the heavenly man (1 Cor 15:49) in a process which has already begun.

The Treasure in Earthen Vessels (4:1– 15)

Paul participates in the transforming ministry of the spirit by the mercy of God. In performing his ministry, Paul has rejected deceitful methods; he does not practice "craftiness or adulterate the word of God" (NASB; see 2:17). Instead, his ministry is an open manifestation of truth (see Gal 2:5) which commends itself to the discerning conscience of people (see 5:11). Paul does not commend himself (3:1; 5:12); he is commended by his message. As every preacher ought to know, method in ministry is determined by message (1 Cor 9:23). In v. 3, Paul takes up the metaphor of the veil again: the veil which was once on the face of Moses, and then over the minds of the Jews, is now covering the eyes of those who hear Paul's preaching. For them, the gospel which promises life has effected judgment, so that they are perishing (see 2:15– 16; 1 Cor 1:18). The minds of these unbelievers have been blinded by "the god of this world," that is, Satan (see 2:11). Paul does not intend to suggest that the blind are not responsible for their unbelief, but that their thoughts are captive to demonic forces. Since they are veiled, the unbelievers are not able to see "the light of the gospel of the glory of Christ" (a text for a sermon). Christ is the content of Paul's gospel, and as a coin bears the impression of the original die, so Christ is stamped with the authentic image of God (see Phil 2:6).

Paul declares, "We do not preach ourselves" (v.5; NASB). Some preachers get in the way of the message. Instead, Paul preaches "Jesus Christ as Lord." The crucified one (1 Cor 2:2) is now proclaimed as exalted Lord of heaven and earth (Phil 2:10–11). Acknowledging that lordship, Paul views himself as servant (Greek: "slave") not only of the Master, but also of those to whom he ministers. The homiletical theme is clear: Christ as Lord; minister as slave. V. 6 suggests a sermon on the relation between creation and redemption. Taking his text from Gen 1:3, Paul declares, "It is God who said, 'Let light shine out of darkness.'" This light of God the Creator is reflected in the face of the Redeemer, Jesus Christ, who reveals God's radiant presence. Through faith in him, the light of God shines in our hearts, not merely to illumine intellect, but also to create a new relationship (see 1 Cor 8:1–2). Creation and redemption come from God; he is the creator of light and the redeemer of life.

No wonder Paul says, "We have this treasure in earthen vessels" (v. 7). By the treasure he means the gospel of Christ; by the earthen vessels—"common clay pots" (TEV)—which can be marred and cracked, he means the ministers. This contrast shows that the power belongs to God, and not to the ministers—a truth to be remembered and preached. Fragile as it is, however, the pottery vessel is not totally shattered: afflicted, not crushed; perplexed, not despairing; persecuted, not forsaken; knocked down, not "knocked out" (Phillips). What holds the earthen vessel together is the treasure it contains— the power of God at work in the frailty of human ministry (12:9). In suffering for the gospel (Phil 3:10), the minister reveals the sacrifice of the crucified Jesus; in constantly being delivered to death (1 Cor 15:31), the minister manifests the life of the risen Christ. Through the death of Christ, the saving power of God's love is disclosed (Rom 5:6–11). Thus, death is at work in Paul, but life is at work in his parishioners.

This risky ministry is grounded in faith. Paul supports his

conviction by a quotation from the Greek translation of the Psalms: "I believed, and so I spoke" (116:10). Paul's exegesis, which displays little interest in the original meaning of the Psalmist, provides the text for a sermon on faith and witness: "We too believe, and so we speak" (v. 13). In other words, the proclamation of the gospel rests on faith in God—a faith confirmed by God's act of raising Christ. On the basis of such faith, one can endure the suffering ministry. Just as life is conveyed to the recipient of the message, so life is promised to the preacher (v. 14).

The Seen and the Unseen (4:16– 5:10)

As he envisages that reality which is beyond death, Paul can repeat his words of 4:1: "We do not lose heart." Paul begins the discussion by presenting a contrast between the "outer nature" and the "inner nature." A distinction between the evil body and the good spirit was common in the hellenistic world. Paul does not share this dualism, but sees human beings—body and spirit—created by God and essentially good. Nevertheless, Paul draws a distinction between the inner person who thinks, feels, wills (Rom 7:22), and the outer body of flesh and blood (1 Cor 15:50) which "is decaying" (v. 16; NASB). Moreover, the inner person, the essential being, has been transformed by the gift of God's spirit (3:18); it is the new creation (5:17) which is "being renewed every day."

In the light of this conception, the sufferings of the present time (vv. 8– 12) appear slight and temporary; they are not to be compared with the coming glory which is already anticipated (see Rom 8:18). This understanding of present troubles is possible for Christians because they view the temporal from the perspective of the eternal—a sermonic theme. Christians do not look to what is seen; they do not fix their lives on transitory things which cannot provide lasting satisfaction. Christians look to the unseen; they focus their vision on the eternal verities of God.

Participation in life beyond death is made possible by "a building from God, a house not made with hands" (5:1). This idea of a dwelling "eternal in the heavens," prepared and waiting for habitation, smacks of Greek philosophical speculation. Its use here indicates that Paul is employing a new metaphor to describe the indescribable. The reality of this expected building stands in contrast to the physical body which is depicted as "an earthly tent." The physical body is temporary and about to be destroyed, that is, it is about to die. Life in this flimsy tent is moved by anxiety and longing in face of the threat of death and in expectation of life in the eternal habitation.

In vv. 2–3 Paul shifts to another metaphor: he speaks of being "clothed with our dwelling from heaven" (NASB). This expression suggests the imagery of donning a heavenly garment. The believer wants to put on this symbolic robe to avoid being "found naked," that is, to avoid the threat of non-being (death). The believer does not "want to have the old body stripped off," but "to have the new body put on over it" (v. 4; NEB). The old body must be transformed into the new, the perishable must put on the imperishable (see 1 Cor 15:51–54).

Preaching from this text should avoid undue complexity. Some commentators suppose Paul is referring to death before the eschaton, while others think he is speaking of the transformation which occurs at the end; still others believe he is describing an intermediate state. Final solutions to problems of this sort are not within our grasp. Paul is sure of one thing—and this we can preach—that God promises a new existence for the person of faith. The metaphors used—dwelling (see John 14:2) and garment (see Rev 16:15)—provide colorful material for homiletical development.

On the basis of this certainty, Paul can say, "We are always of good courage" (5:6). This courage, as v. 8 makes clear, is inspired by the hope of being with the Lord. In this life in the body, the believer is not fully united with Christ (Rom 6:5); "we are exiles from the Lord" (NEB). In this bodily existence, "we walk by faith, not by sight"—a basic Pauline idea and an appropriate text for preaching. Most people do not want to walk by faith; they prefer secure steps and rigid rules. People of faith, on the other hand, do not see precisely where they are going; they hope for the unseen (Rom 8:24).

If Paul had his choice, he would "rather be away from the body and at home with the Lord" (see Phil 1:23). Death held no threat for him; instead, it offered the promise of Christ's presence (see Rom 14:8). The only issue, then, is this: whether we live or die "we make it our aim to please him" (v. 9). The effort to please is grounded in the gracious presence of Christ, but his stern call to obedience must not be ignored (see Rom 2:16). Every believer must face an ultimate accounting, and receive recompense for "what he has done in the body" (v. 10). This idea that judgment is on the basis of what one has done (see Rom 2:6) does not mean Paul has abandoned his doctrine of justification by faith (Rom 3:21– 26). Although one comes into right relationship with God on the ground of faith, that relationship makes possible good works.

The Ministry of Reconciliation (5:11– 6:10)

The certainty of judgment prompts Paul to speak of the "fear of the Lord"—an OT theme (see Deut 10:12) which stresses awesome responsibility in the presence of God (Rom 11:20; Phil 2:12). The truth about the ministry is "made manifest to God" (v. 11; NASB), and this truth appeals to the conscience of Christians as well (see 4:2). Paul does not consider this claim to constitute another attempt at commending himself (3:1; 4:2), but to afford the Corinthians an opportunity to be proud of their ministers. This appropriate pride (contrast 1 Cor 1:12) can provide an answer to Paul's critics who are concerned about externals (see 10:10) rather than the heart (see 1 Sam 16:7). Perhaps pulpit committees function in a similar fashion today, measuring ministers by quantifiable credentials, rather than by the inner qualities which are recognized by God. In his reckless abandon to the concerns of God, Paul appears to be beside himself, a fool "for Christ's sake" (1 Cor 4:10). In his dealing with parishioners, however, Paul is in his right mind. His ministry is a model of clarity of speech (1 Cor 14:6– 12) and integrity of conduct (4:2). In all things, "the love of Christ controls us" (v. 14). This love becomes the guiding force for ministerial practice and ethical behavior—and a text for preaching. As sacrifice which reveals God's love (Rom 5:8), Christ died on behalf of us all (see v. 21), and through unity with his death (Rom 6:3– 4; Gal 2:20), we have all died to ourselves. Since we have died with Christ, we cannot serve our own interests, but live in response to him who died and was raised on our behalf.

The result is a new situation in which "worldly standards have ceased to count in our estimate" of any person (v. 16; NEB). A sermon would be possible on the theme: the new perspective of faith. Through the eyes of faith, all things appear as new. Even Christ, whom Paul once viewed as stumbling-block and foolishness, is now recognized as the power and wisdom of God (1 Cor 1:23– 24). Through faith in him, all persons are being transformed (3:18) into new creatures (see Gal 6:15). The process of transformation is described in this text in terms of Paul's doctrine of reconciliation (see Rom 5:10). Of all Paul's metaphors of salvation, reconciliation may be the easiest for moderns to appreciate, and therefore, the most fruitful for preaching. The terms "reconcile" and "reconciliation" can be used for personal relationships which are common to our experience. Persons who are alienated from one another can be reconciled; the relationship of enmity can be overcome in a relationship which restores an original harmony. Paul can use this terminology to describe the reconciliation between husband and wife (1 Cor 7:11). In the apocrypha, the idea that people engage in religious practices in order to reconcile God to themselves is emphasized (2 Macc 1:5; 7:32; 8:29). Paul turns this understanding inside out: Instead of people reconciling God to themselves, God reconciles people to himself. Vv. 18– 19 contain three parallel elements which develop Paul's doctrine:

(1) All this is from God
(2) who through Christ reconciled us to himself
(3) and gave us the ministry of reconciliation;

(1) God
(2) in Christ was reconciling the world to himself,
(3) and entrusting to us the message of reconciliation.

These elements make the following points: (1) God is the source and primary agent of reconciliation. (2) The means of reconciliation is Christ; reconciliation is an act of God's love which forgives, which does not "count their trespasses against them" (v. 19). (3) God's reconciling action is communicated through the message and ministry of reconciliation.

Entrusted with the message of reconciliation, ministers— indeed, all Christians—become "ambassadors for Christ" (v. 20). Like ambassadors, they act not on their own authority, but on behalf of the power they represent. This sermonic theme can be developed by noting that God actually makes "his appeal through us;" the reconciling activity of God is communicated through the witness of believers. On behalf of Christ, ministers can declare: "Be reconciled to God." But how, if all is from God, can preachers confront the hearers with an imperative? The answer is: God's gift of reconciliation must be received by a free and responsible decision (see Phil 2:12– 13).

Above all, reconciliation is possible because of God's action in the crucifixion. "Christ was innocent of sin, and yet for our sake God made him one with the sinfulness of men, so that in him we might be made one with the goodness of God himself" (v. 21; NEB)—a difficult, but preachable text. God sent his son "in the likeness of sinful flesh" (Rom 8:3), but Jesus did not engage in the sort of disobedience which characterizes human sin. The identification with sinful humanity, real in the incarnation, becomes complete in the crucifixion. There Christ is fully identified with the sin of mankind; there he has "become a curse for us"(Gal 3:13; see Mark 15:34). This identification means that reconciling love is not a vague hypothesis, but an actual event in the life of God.

"Sharing in God's work," Paul urges the Corinthians who have received God's grace not to "let it go for nothing" (6:1; NEB). To make his point, Paul quotes Isa 49:8—a text which refers to the time when God will save his people. According to the OT text, that time would be the "day of salvation" at the end of history. Paul's exegesis is striking: the day of salvation is not future, but now. This "now" is the "now" of preaching—the present time when reconciliation is offered and received.

The message of reconciliation is the announcement of the eschatological event; it is God's powerful action for salvation (Rom 1:16). In view of this ultimate dimension, Paul's sufferings for the gospel lose their threat. In face of such things, Paul is armed with "weapons of righteousness" (v. 7; 10:4)—"purity, knowledge, forbearance"(v. 6), etc. Life in service of the gospel is depicted in a portrait of contrasts (vv. 9– 10; see 1 Cor 4:10– 13). The minister is unrecognized by people (1 Cor 1:26), but known to God (1 Cor 8:3; Gal 4:9); subjected to death (4:10– 11), yet possessing life (5:4– 5); sharing sorrows, yet rejoicing always (1 Thess 5:16); owning nothing, yet inheriting the riches of God (1 Cor 3:21).

Open Hearts and Restricted Affections (6:11 – 7:4)

On the basis of this ministry, Paul makes an appeal to the Corinthians. The appeal is interrupted at v. 14. The material of 6:14 – 7:1 appears to be out of place, since it has no obvious connection with what comes before, and since the argument seems to move directly from 6:13 to 7:2. Some scholars believe this material originally belonged to another Pauline composition, perhaps the "previous letter" mentioned in 1 Cor 5:9 (see Intro.). I think it is better, however, to consider 6:14 – 7:1 a non-Pauline fragment which has been mistakenly inserted here.

Regardless of the authenticity of the passage, 6:14 – 7:1 provides the occasion for discussion and preaching on the theme: the relation of Christians to the world. The text begins, "Do not harness yourselves in an uneven team with unbelievers" (JB)—an expression reminiscent of the OT prohibition against yoking unlike animals together (Deut 22:10). Paul appears to be less restrictive than the author of this passage, since he allows Christians to remain married to unbelievers (1 Cor 7:12 – 16). However, he does believe that a sharp line ought to be drawn between church and world, insisting that Christian worship excludes participation in pagan ritual (1 Cor 10:21).

The author of 6:14 – 7:1 develops his understanding of the exclusions by a series of questions: "What partnership have righteousness and iniquity? What fellowship has light with darkness?" etc. The ground on which he bases the demands for exclusiveness is solid: Believers "are the temple of the living God" (see 1 Cor 3:16; 6:19). The church is depicted as God's dwelling place, and as such it must be holy. The author supports this conviction by a collection of OT references. First, he shows, employing texts like Lev 26:12 and Ezek 37:27, that God has a special relation to his people. Then, on the basis of this relationship, the author affirms God's call to come out and be separate (see Isa 52:11; Jer 51:45). If listeners will heed this call to separation and holiness, then an intimate relationship between God and his people will be manifest: he will be their father and they will be his sons and daughters (Ezek 20:34 and 2 Sam 7:14). The passage ends with an admonition on the basis of these OT precepts: "Let us therefore cleanse ourselves from all that can defile flesh or spirit, and in the fear of God complete our consecration" (NEB).

Paul's appeal to the Corinthians (6:11–13+7:2–4) is moved by personal concerns. This is seen in his shift to first-person singular in vv. 3–4. He begins the appeal with a description of the open style of his ministry: "We have spoken very frankly to you; we have opened our heart wide to you all" (6:11; NEB). This openness of ministry places no restriction upon the Corinthians. Instead, it encourages them to respond in like fashion, to "widen your hearts also." If there is any restriction on the recipients of Paul's ministry, it is self-imposed. "You are restricted in your own affections"—a truth about "up-tight" persons which may be a text for a sermon. The grace of God functioning in openness of ministry evokes an open response—a flexibility in life-style characterized by the warmth of human affection.

Paul offers this advice as a loving parent: "I speak as if to children of mine" (v. 13; JB). Nothing in Paul's ministry should keep the Corinthians from opening their heart in affection to their ministers. "We have taken advantage of no one" (see 12:17). On the contrary, Paul sees himself in close personal relationship with his parishioners: they are "in our hearts" (see 3:2); with the ministers, they share death and life (see 4:14).

This is the sort of intimate oneness within the church which should inform our preaching on Christian unity. In contrast to their criticism, Paul has confidence in the Corinthians and boasts of their faithfulness (7:14; see 1 Thess 2:19). This pride and confidence fills Paul with comfort (see 7:6). Thus, in the midst of affliction (1:8; 6:4), Paul is "overflowing with joy" (v. 4; NASB). Modern Christians can be instructed by this model: in the face of intense suffering (see 11:24–28), one can say, "Rejoice always" (1 Thess 5:16).

Comfort at the Coming of Titus

(2 Corinthians 7:5–16)

At v. 5, Paul returns to the account of his trip to Macedonia (2:13). When he arrived there from Troas, he was deeply troubled; "we were harassed at every turn" (NIV). The afflictions which he endured (see 1:4) affected his total person— "fighting without and fear within." The coming of Titus overcame this inward and outward anxiety. Yet, it was not really Titus who comforted him, but "God who comforts the downcast"—an appropriate text for a sermon on the comforting concern of God (see 1:3–4; Isa 40:1; 49:13). As Paul has become aware of God's comfort through his meeting with Titus, so Titus had been comforted by his experience with the Corinthians. They had convinced him of their concern for Paul. This gratifying report, in face of the stormy relations of the past, encourages Paul to rejoice.

Prior to their expression of concern, the Corinthians had been made sorrowful by a letter which Paul had written them. Paul, for a time, had regretted sending the letter, because it has caused the Corinthians pain. Now, in the light of Titus' report, he does not regret the letter, since the pain was temporary and the result good: the sorrow which the letter evoked led to repentance. Paul's letter, seemingly detrimental, proved to be beneficial to the Corinthians, "so you are no losers by what we did" (v. 9; NEB).

I believe a sermon is suggested by v. 10 on the theme: Godly sorrow and the sorrow of the world. The grief of the world—"the hurt which is borne in the world's way" (NEB)— leads to death. A sorrow which cannot cope with its origin, which is weighed down with guilt, which cannot be cured by worldly remedies, underscores the frailty of human existence. The sorrow which responds to God, which is sensitive to his judging and redemptive power, leads to repentance, and finally to salvation (Rom 2:4).

As well as being comforted by the response of the Corinthians, Paul is "especially delighted" (v. 13; NIV) by the news of Titus' reception in Corinth. Titus had been sent to Corinth, perhaps with the severe letter. Knowing the tensions which existed between Paul and the church, Titus no doubt approached Corinth with considerable trepidation. As it turned out, the Corinthians "helped put his mind at ease" (NIV), so that he was able to rejoice. When Titus recalls the welcome he received, "his affection for you is all the greater" (v. 15; NIV). The reception included a willingness to obey the apostolic instruction which Titus conveyed, and an attitude characterized by the OT virtue of "fear and trembling" (Ps 119:120; Jer 33:9). Paul's use of this theme could provide the basis for a sermon, since "fear and trembling" characterizes a style of ministry (1 Cor 2:3), an attitude of response (2 Cor 7:15), and a quest for salvation (Phil 2:12). There may be a lesson here, too, for church administrators concerned with conflict management. When two persons or groups anticipate a serious confrontation, both sides come with fear. An attitude of acceptance and openness can overcome that; "perfect love casts out fear" (1 John 4:18).

The Collection for the Saints
(2 Corinthians 8:1–9:15)

The Grace of God and the Gifts of the Christian
(8:1–24)

Paul turns to the question of the offering for the Christians of Jerusalem. The collecting of the offering had been pledged by Paul at the Jerusalem conference (Gal 2:10), and had been discussed with the Corinthians in 1 Cor 16:1–4. As 2 Cor 8 and 9 indicate, the task of collection had not been brought to successful completion in Corinth. Paul's advice on the matter provides the preacher with texts which are helpful for addressing the budgetary and benevolent concerns of the congregation.

Paul begins his instruction by focusing attention on the example of the Macedonians. He views the response of their churches (probably Philippi and Thessalonica) as a sign of the grace of God. In response to God's grace, the Macedonians have acted in generosity toward their fellow-Christians of Jerusalem. This is especially noteworthy, because the Macedonians had experienced affliction (Phil 1:29; 1 Thess 1:6; 2:14; 3:3), and were not noted for their affluence. As a matter of fact, they gave out of "their rock-bottom poverty" (v. 2; Barrett), giving not only "according to their means," but even "beyond their ability" (NASB). The Macedonians had "urgently pleaded with us for the privilege of sharing in this service to the saints" (v. 4; NIV). Surely, the Macedonians provide a model for the Corinthians, and for modern Christians, too; they do the unexpected. The most important feature of their example becomes a text for our preaching: "first they gave themselves to the Lord" (v. 5). The Macedonians had their priorities straight! When Christians give themselves to Christ, their gifts to meet the needs of others follow spontaneously.

Titus is to play an important role in the completion of the collection. I believe an imaginative sermon could be devel-

oped on the career of Titus as the faithful worker who is as-
signed trying tasks. According to Galatians, he had been taken
by Paul to the Jerusalem conference to prove that uncircumcised Greeks could be Christians (2:1, 3). Apparently, he had
been sent to Corinth, some time after the writing of 1 Corinthians, to begin the collection (2 Cor 8:6; 12:18). Still later, he
had been given the distressing assignment of delivering the severe letter (2:4; 7:8). Now he is about to be sent to Corinth to
complete the collection of an offering which has proved to be
something less than popular, and to our surprise, he is willing
to go "of his own accord." As any senior minister knows, associates like that are hard to find!

Paul bases his appeal to the Corinthians on a variety of
motives. Since they have been enriched with gifts (1 Cor 1:5),
they ought to "excel in this gracious work also" (v. 7). The
word translated "gracious work" is *charis* or "grace"; as
Christians have received grace, so they should act in grace.
The response of grace is not a matter of command, but of free
will. It is moved by love exemplified by others (like the
Macedonians) and responsive to a gracious ministry (like
Paul's). Most of all, generous giving is grounded in the deed of
God, revealed in Christ (v. 9).

Here is the Christo-centric basis for our efforts to raise the
budget and promote benevolence. The riches and poverty of
Christ depict the condescension of the pre-existent one who
assumed the form of a servant (Phil 2:6–8). Through this poverty, believers have been enriched by the forgiving grace of
God, "as having nothing, and yet possessing everything"
(6:10). In response to that gift, they should give generously to
the Christians of Judaea. The reality of the incarnation underscores the "materialism" of Christianity; spiritual blessings
take material, even monetary, form.

Paul's opinion (see 1 Cor 7:25) is that the Corinthians
should complete the collection which they had begun a year
ago. No doubt he thinks they have been dragging their feet.
They had begun, perhaps grudgingly, to do the work, but did
not have the desire to carry it through to completion. The
Corinthians should now give of their abundance to alleviate
the poverty of the Judaeans, for if the circumstances should be
reversed, the Judaeans would be able to share the burdens of
the Corinthians. The Corinthian church, though not noted for

its wealth (1 Cor 1:26), did have affluent members like "Erastus, the city treasurer" (Rom 16:23) and the people who hosted the excessive observances of the Lord's Supper (1 Cor 11:17–22). Scriptural sanction is given to the idea of equality among the people of God by reference to the gathering of manna in the wilderness (Exod 16:18). By some strange mystery in the economy of God, those who gathered more than they needed had nothing in excess, while those who did not gather enough did not lack for food.

Paul is thankful that God has put a concern for the Corinthians in the heart of Titus. He has been asked by Paul to serve in the completing of the collection, and is eager on his own accord to return to Corinth. Along with Titus, Paul is sending "the brother who is famous among all the churches for his preaching of the gospel"(v. 18)—a reputation worth emulating. Since Paul's letters were probably read before the churches, he may have assumed that Titus would introduce this otherwise unknown brother to the congregation at this point in the reading. In any case, this famous preacher has been appointed by the churches (Greek: by a show of hands) to accompany Paul in the administration of the collection. This "gracious work," though it meets the needs of people, is ultimately to the "glory of the Lord," as is all authentic giving. Delegates of the churches are taken along "to guard against any criticism of our handling of this generous gift" (v. 20, NEB; see 1 Cor 16:3). With Titus and the brother, Paul is sending another unnamed delegate.

God's Gift and Christian Generosity (9:1–15)

In chap 9, Paul continues the discussion of the offering for Jerusalem. Just as Paul had boasted to the Corinthians about the generosity of the Macedonians (8:1–5), now he reports his boasting about the Corinthians to his hosts in Macedonia. Apparently, Paul is willing to appeal to the motive of "healthy competition" (see Rom 12:10) in promoting the collection.

The extending of the concern into chap. 9 shows how seriously Paul views the offering for the Jerusalem saints (i.e. Christians). Although he says it is superfluous to write, he betrays his own misgivings by writing anyway. I think there is a sermon here: how much of the preaching and teaching of the church is superfluous, repeating what Christians ought already to know and do! Paul's boasting in the readiness of the Corinthians to contribute has been optimistic, since he knows that the work begun a year ago has not yet been brought to completion (8:10– 11). Thus, his boasting becomes a lever to move the Corinthians. When the brethren (Titus and the two delegates mentioned in 8:16– 23) arrive, they will be able to see if Paul's boasting is well-founded. When Paul arrives later, possibly accompanied by Macedonians, he—not to mention the Corinthians—could be humiliated by Corinthian failure to complete the collection. After all, the Corinthians had promised the gift, and Paul hopes they will offer it willingly, "not as something wrung from you" (v. 5; Barrett).

In v. 6, Paul introduces the symbol of sowing and reaping—a common metaphor of hellenistic literature (see Gal 6:7). On the surface, Paul appears to be saying that those who give generously will be rewarded abundantly. Actually, Paul believes generosity will produce divine blessings which will permit further generosity. In response to your giving, God will so provide that "you will have ample means in yourselves to meet each and every situation, with enough and to spare for every good cause" (v. 8; NEB). Ps 112:9 views the benevolence of one who gives to the poor as a sign of his righteousness. Texts like Isa 55:10 and Hos 10:12 indicate that God who "supplies seed to the sower and bread for food will supply and multiply your resources and increase the harvest of your righteousness" (v. 10). In other words, God provides the resources for a generosity which serves to demonstrate one's righteousness. The reward for generosity is the provision for more generosity, offered not in self-interest, but to "produce thanksgiving to God" (v. 11). The sermonic theme is: enriched for generosity. Paul, out of his experience of poverty (see Phil 4:11– 12), surely knows that there are situations in which one does not seem "rich enough to be generous" (v. 10; NEB). This simply shows how much generosity depends on God's grace—not our ability—and how truly, in the economy of God, the believer who has received God's gift is able to give (see Acts 3:6).

Paul also presents the theme: God's grace and free-will giving. In response to God's free gift, one must make up one's own mind; giving in response to grace cannot be "under compulsion" (v. 7). Indeed, the gift should be accompanied by joy.

This attitude is approved by God who "loves a cheerful giver"—a sermonic text.

Throughout this paragraph various motives for benevolence are mentioned which may serve as an outline for a sermon: (1) it will benefit the giver as "the harvest of your righteousness" (v. 10); (2) it will benefit the recipients by "supplying the needs of the saints" (v. 12; NASB); (3) it will work for the mutual benefit of giver and receiver by creating a relationship wherein "they long for you and pray for you" (v. 14); (4) it will "benefit" God by offering him thanksgiving (v. 12) and glorifying him (v. 13). The sermon's title could be (if you're not too squeamish about alliteration): "The Benefits of Benevolence."

Giving is also put in new perspective by v. 12, where Paul describes the collection of the offering as "the ministry of this service" (NASB). The word translated "service" is the Greek term *leitourgia* or "liturgy." Thus, giving is understood as a "liturgy"—as a way of worship (see Rom 12:1) in which thanksgiving and glory to God can be expressed. Giving is also related to one's "confession of the gospel of Christ" (v. 13; NIV). The good news is not simply to be heard; it is to be obeyed in an obedience which takes the shape of concrete acts of love.

The message of chaps 8 and 9 reaches its climax in v. 15: "Thanks be to God for his inexpressible gift." This is a basic text for all our giving—and living. The gift is the grace of God mentioned in the preceding verse, and the content of the gift is Jesus Christ. The word translated "inexpressible" or "indescribable" is used nowhere else in the NT. Though rare in Greek literature, the term can refer to a wonder which is beyond description. The gift of Christ defies description. The magnitude of his love (Rom 8:35), the perfection of his obedience (Phil 2:8), the power of his risen presence (Phil 3:10)—none of this can be described by objective data or doctrinal formulation. Yet, the preacher is called to this incredible duty: to describe the indescribable.

In Defense of Ministry
(2 Corinthians 10:1–13:10)

Boasting in the Lord (10:1– 18)

At 10:1, there is an abrupt change in the tone of Paul's argument. Most scholars agree that chaps. 10– 13 belong to a different letter (see Intro.). In these chapters, Paul is engaged in defense of his apostleship against attacks which have been launched by opponents. Along the way, Paul discloses some fascinating autobiographical data which serves both to underscore his humanness and to inspire beleaguered ministers of every generation.

This section of the letter begins with an appeal based on "the meekness and gentleness of Christ." Our preaching, too, could appeal to the example of Christ, who emptied himself to take on the form of a servant (Phil 2:7). In response to this humility, the Corinthians ought to be more humble in their criticism of Paul, though he himself will be something less than a model of meekness in his treatment of them. Apparently, the charge has been made that Paul is humble when present, and bold when absent—timid in personal relations, daring in his letters (10:9– 10). As a matter of practice, Paul would prefer to assume a pastoral style in his personal dealings with his parishioners (see 1 Cor 4:21); he writes potent messages in his epistles to avoid the necessity of severity in direct confrontation (13:10). However, if need be, "I could put on as bold a face as you please against those who charge us with moral weakness"(v. 2; NEB).

Literally, the charge is that Paul "walks according to the flesh." This may indicate that his opponents, like the pious elite of our own time, claim that they are walking by the spirit. In his defense, Paul admits that he lives in the world. Nevertheless, Paul does not engage in a worldly war; his battle has to do with the unseen matters of ultimate importance (4:18). His weapons are not the instruments of the world's power, but spiritual armaments (see 1 Thess 5:8). These weap-

ons, concealed under the weakness with which Paul is charged
(see 11:29), "have divine power to destroy strongholds" (see
12:9).

A sermon on "the weapons of our warfare" could be developed along the lines of Paul's explication of the Christian conflict. According to Paul, the Christian offensive involves three
strategic actions: (1) "We demolish arguments and every pre-
tension that sets itself up against the knowledge of God" (v. 5;
NIV); the primary objective in the Christian struggle is the
recognition of the reality of God. (2) "We compel every human
thought to surrender in obedience to Christ" (NEB); victory in
the Christian battle demands confession of the lordship of
Christ. (3) "We are prepared to punish all rebellion when once
you have put yourselves in our hands" (NEB); enlistment in
the army of the Lord requires obedience, discipline, and
judgment.

The need for obedience is demonstrated by the behavior
of the Corinthians. They "are looking only on the surface of
things" (v. 7; NIV). They have been led astray by opponents of
Paul who claim to have an exclusive relation with Christ (see 1
Cor 1:12). Paul can make the same claim with confidence, and
beyond that, he can boast in his authority as an apostle (1 Cor
9:1). This authority has been given him by the Lord (Gal 1:12)
for the building up and not the tearing down of the church
(13:10). The stern assertion of that authority in his letters is
not designed to frighten his readers. They have charged, "His
letters are weighty and strong, but his bodily presence is
weak, and his speech *(logos)* is of no account" (v. 10). The latter phrase gives me comfort; if Paul's auditors thought his
word was of no account, critics of my preaching can be endured! Paul's opponents, however, were not describing his
powerful message (1 Cor 2:3–4; 1 Thess 1:5; 2:13), but his patient, pastoral style. All that is about to change. When he
comes again (see 13:2), Paul will make it clear that what he
writes when absent, he will practice when present.

In asserting his authority, Paul does not intend to class or
compare himself with "those who commend themselves" (v.
12). These opponents of Paul make extravagant claims about
their relation to Christ (v. 7). As evidence of their folly, "they
measure themselves by themselves, to find in themselves their
own standard of comparison" (NEB). A meditation for Chris-

tian leaders could be developed on the theme: "standards for service." Do you measure your ministry by human standards, or by "the measure of the stature of the fullness of Christ" (Eph 4:13).

Paul appears to move from the question of limiting his boasting to a discussion of the geographical limits of his mission. Apparently, the discussion results from the fact that Corinth has been invaded by competing missionaries from the outside. As well as overextending themselves into the sphere of Paul's mission, these opponents have claimed the results of his work as sign of their own success. Paul, by way of contrast, was the first to come all the way to Corinth with the gospel. He hopes that their faith will be so strengthened that he will have the freedom to "preach the gospel in lands beyond you" (v. 16). Paul's strategy is to work where Christ has never been preached (see Rom 15:20). Above all, he will not boast in work which has already been done in someone else's territory. Every kind of ministerial boasting—even his own (v. 13)—is risky, and needs to heed the scriptural admonition: "Let him who boasts, boast in the Lord" (Jer 9:24; 1 Cor 1:31). Rather than commending themselves, as Paul's opponents do (v. 12), faithful ministers are commended by the Lord. God sets the standards.

Masquerading as Apostles (11:1–15)

Although Paul does not want to engage in boasting, he is driven to it by his opponents (see 12:11). The act of boasting can be characterized as "foolishness"—a theme which is played with variations throughout chaps. 11 and 12. Paul begins the discussion with a plea for his hearers to "put up with a little of my foolishness" (NIV). His desire to gain a hearing is moved by his jealous concern for the Corinthians. Borrowing a metaphor from marriage, Paul says, "I betrothed you to Christ to present you as a pure bride to her one husband." In using this imagery, Paul depicts himself as the father of the bride; the act of betrothal symbolized his founding of the Corinthian church (see 1 Cor 4:15). The resolve of the father is to give away the betrothed daughter as a "chaste virgin" (JB) to the bridegroom; Paul's intent is to present the church in its purity to Christ (see 4:14; Col 1:22). Sermons on the "jealousy of God" (stressing the particularity of God's love) and the "purity of the church" (emphasizing its faithfulness to Christ) could be developed. Just as Eve was deceived and, according to Jewish legend, seduced by the serpent, so the Corinthians have been "led astray from a sincere and pure devotion to Christ" (v. 3).

The infidelity of the Corinthians is disclosed by the way they welcome heretical missionaries "with open arms" (v. 4; JB). In 11:4, the heresy is characterized by three marks which may provide an outline for a sermon. Although heresy hunting should be perpetrated with caution, faithful preaching of the gospel in our time cannot keep silence in the face of phony faiths which beguile our people. The marks are: (1) preaching another Jesus, (2) offering another spirit, (3) presenting another gospel. The criterion for judging these errors is the apostolic witness on which the church is built (1 Cor 3:11). The authentic Jesus is the crucified Christ (1 Cor 1:23); the true spirit confesses Jesus as Lord (1 Cor 12:3); the genuine gospel re-presents God's redemptive action in Christ (Gal 3:1). The criterion is not fancy rhetoric nor the mastery of the media—the performance of "a polished speechmaker" (v. 6; JB; see 1 Cor 2:4); the criterion is knowledge—the content of the message, grounded in sound theology (see 10:5). Thus, for all the rhetorical skill of his opponents, Paul is not inferior to these proud pretenders who by their showy deception purport to be "superlative apostles."

Just as Paul's untutored rhetoric does not disqualify his ministry, neither does his practice of preaching the gospel "free of charge" (v. 7; NIV). Apparently, Paul's foes have argued that his failure to accept support from the Corinthians is proof that his preaching isn't worth much. Employing sharp irony, Paul asks if it is a sin for him "to lower myself in order to elevate you" (NIV)—an act which imitates the condescension of Christ (8:9). Paul had refused financial support (1 Cor 9:12), and had supported his mission in Corinth by practicing his trade (see Acts 18:3; 1 Thess 2:9). Paul's trade must not have proved sufficiently lucrative, since his "needs were supplied by the brethren who came from Macedonia" (v. 9; see Phil 4:16). By accepting their "support" (a military term which can be used for a soldier's rations; 1 Cor 9:7), Paul says ironically that he "robbed other churches." This probably implies that the Macedonians had little to spare, and that Paul's needs were serious. Regardless of his need, Paul was not a burden (see 1 Thess 2:9); "if I ran short I sponged on no one (v. 9; NEB). In no case, will his boasting about his financial independence be silenced—a conviction confirmed by an oath (v. 10; contrast Matt 5:34–37).

His unwillingness to accept support, however, should not be construed to mean that he does not love the Corinthians. On the contrary, his love for them has been demonstrated in a host of ways (1 Cor 4:14; 16:24) and is attested by God. His refusal to accept monetary assistance, however, will "cut the ground from under those who would seize any chance to put their vaunted apostleship on the same level as ours" (v. 12; NEB). Paul's opponents, no doubt, have been accepting offerings—a right which Paul basically approves (1 Cor 9:3–14). Nevertheless, to put themselves on his level of ministry—to abandon a self-serving right in order to assume the role of a slave (4:5)—this is a challenge too high for the "super-apostles" (v. 5; NIV).

In vv. 12–15, Paul's counterattack on the invading missionaries becomes severe. He describes them as "counterfeit" (JB) or "sham apostles, crooked in all their practices, masquerading as apostles of Christ" (NEB). This deceitful masquerade is not surprising, since "Satan disguises himself as an angel of light" (v. 14). According to Jewish legend, Satan assumed the radiant guise of an angel when he came to deceive Eve. Since Satan wears disguises, it is no big deal (Greek: no great thing) when "his servants masquerade as servants of righteousness" (v. 15; NIV). Those who preach another Jesus are not simply mistaken; they are demonic. "They will meet the end their deeds deserve" (NEB; see Phil 3:19; 1 Thess 2:16). The deceptive style of Paul's opponents has been duplicated by later generations; demons have their disciples, false causes their champions, all masquerading as ministers of light. That is why heretics are often hard to recognize; it is not easy to tell demons from angels. Paul resembles neither (see 10:10); he bears on his body "the marks of Jesus" (Gal 6:17).

Boasting in Weakness (11:16–33)

In v. 16, Paul repeats the theme of foolishness (11:1). Although he should not be considered foolish, Paul's boasting is a form of folly. Thus, if the Corinthians think him foolish, they ought to accept him as a fool, that is, listen to his "insane" (v. 23; NASB) boasting. Throughout the paragraph Paul is apologetic about his boasts, repeatedly describing his speech as senseless (vv. 17, 21, 23). His boasting is not "with the Lord's authority" (see 1 Cor 7:25), but according to his own "boastful confidence." I believe a sermon could consider the question, What are you proud of? Paul says many boast "of worldly things" (Greek: "according to the flesh"; see 5:16), while others glory in spiritual matters (visions and revelations; 12:1). When "talking like a madman" (v. 23), Paul can boast of these things, too. When he is in his right mind (see 5:13), he boasts "of things that show my weakness" (v. 30); such boasting does not represent pride in himself, but in the power of Christ (12:8– 10; see 10:17).

The Corinthians ought to be able to put up with Paul's foolishness (11:1), since they "gladly bear with fools, being wise" themselves (v. 19). This ironical exclamation implies that Paul's opponents are the real fools (see 11:21), and the gullible Corinthians, who pride themselves on wisdom (1 Cor 4:10), are the biggest fools of all. Evidence of their folly is the readiness of the Corinthians to put up with anything. "If a man tyrannizes over you, exploits you, gets you in his clutches, puts on airs, and hits you in the face, you put up with it" (v. 20; NEB). Some of this description may characterize the behavior of the opponents who may have exploited the Corinthian hospitality, eating "you out of house and home" (Barrett). A sermon could address the theme: "what people will put up with." In our time, people complain about the church—its captivity to culture, the dullness of its worship—but they willingly endure the tedium of modern existence—its bondage to gadgets, the trivia of its entertainment. They should be encouraged to put up with some real foolishness—the stumbling block of the cross (1 Cor 1:23).

Paul's foolish boasting becomes more realistic in vv. 22– 23. There he engages in comparison with his opponents (see 10:12). The assertion that they are Hebrews indicates that the opponents (or their backers) have been born into a particular ethnic group. The claim that they are Israelites means that they belong to the chosen people of God. The affirmation that they are "descendants of Abraham" implies that they are heirs of the ancient faith. Paul does not contest these claims;

he simply replies, "Me too" (see Phil 3:5). What is at stake is the opponents' claim that they are "servants of Christ" (v. 23). Although Paul does not directly deny that claim (see 10:7), he disqualifies it by setting criteria which the opponents do not acknowledge. As to being a servant of Christ, Paul asserts—in a foolish outburst which belies the humility of Christ—"I am a better one." Proof that he is a better servant (Greek: *diakonos*; see 6:4–10) rests on the evidence that he works harder (see 1 Cor 15:10) and endures more (1 Cor 4:9–13) than his opponents. In a summary which makes the trials recorded in Acts seem puny by comparison, Paul lists "far more imprisonments" (Acts 16:24) and exposure "to death again and again" (NIV; see 1:9).

In vv. 24–29, Paul presents a vignette of his suffering ministry. He begins by offering details of his "countless beatings" mentioned in v. 23. The penalty of "forty lashes less one" remembers the OT provision for forty punitive stripes "but not more" (Deut 25:3). To avoid a miscount, the Jews restricted the flogging to thirty-nine. Paul (who apparently continued to submit to synagogue jurisdiction) was probably charged with associating with Gentiles or eating forbidden food (Gal 2:12; 1 Cor 8:8; 10:25–27). Reference to being "beaten with rods" describes a Roman punishment which Paul suffered at Philippi (Acts 16:22–23). Paul's crime, in the eyes of the Romans, would probably have been his disrupting of the public order (see Acts 17:6).

The portrait of Paul, frequently sentenced to severe punishment, hardly reflects a theological recluse who restricted his activity to prayer and meditation! The reference to stoning confirms the incredible incident at Lystra (Acts 14:19). Although Acts has mentioned no shipwrecks to this point in his career, Paul's extensive missionary activity has required frequent travel by sea. Paul has also undertaken "frequent journeys" on land, which, in spite of the Roman peace and the Roman roads, were fraught with perils. As well as the threat of robbers, Paul faces danger from his "own people" (the Jews), from those to whom his mission is directed (the Gentiles), and from "false brethren" (heretical Christians like those faced at Corinth).

As well as danger, Paul has to endure the privations of an arduous ministry: "toil and hardship," sleepless nights, "hun-

ger and thirst . . . cold and exposure" (v. 27). "Anxious concern
for all our congregations" (NEB) weighs heavily upon him every day. When one of the members is weak, Paul shares that
weakness (see 1 Cor 9:22). When one parishioner is caused to
stumble, Paul is consumed with indignation. This catalog of
hardships represents the weakness of which Paul boasts, and
though the data may seem incredible, God is Paul's witness
that he does not lie. In all of this, Paul presents a model of ministry which too few of us emulate. The climactic example of
weakness is his humiliating escape from Damascus (see Acts
9:24–25). While Paul considers this and the other incidents of
the catalog to be signs of his weakness, the perceptive reader
is impressed by another factor: the strength of Paul's endurance. The weakness of which he boasts, like the weakness of
the crucified Christ (1 Cor 1:25; 2 Cor 13:4), is a paradoxical
display of power (see 12:10).

Visions, Revelations, and Signs of an Apostle (12:1–13)

Having boasted of his weakness, Paul proceeds to mention his "visions and revelations." He must boast about such
things because the Corinthians have "forced me to it" (v. 11;
see 11:30). Although "it does no good," Paul decides to describe ecstatic experiences which have been "granted by the
Lord" (NEB). Actually, he presents only one, and has to reach
back fourteen years into the past to come up with that; religious ecstasy is not a regular feature of Paul's spiritual life
(see 1 Cor 14:18–19).

His recollection of the experience, however, provides an
instructive guide for modern followers of the spiritual quest.
For one thing, Paul is modest about his spiritual accomplish-
ments; he describes himself in the third person as "a man in
Christ." Also, Paul has little interest in the mechanics of
spirituality, the techniques of meditation; he doesn't know or
care whether he was "in the body or out of the body." Finally,
Paul observes the private nature of religious experience. Rather than inflicting some special revelation on the spiritually
uninitiated, Paul "heard words so secret that human lips may
not repeat them" (v. 5; NEB). The communication of secret
doctrine was a typical feature of the hellenistic cults, and so
also was the experience of flight into the third (highest) heav-

en where paradise was located. While paraphernalia of this sort belong to the worldview of the first century, they are hardly at home in the cosmology of the twentieth. Much modern spirituality is irrelevant.

About "this man" of spiritual experience, Paul will boast, "but on my own behalf I will not boast, except of my weaknesses" (v. 5). Paul can boast about the spiritual man because that boasting communicates no public information which can confirm his ministry (v. 4). Like speaking in tongues, spiritual ecstasy is a matter for private consumption (1 Cor 14:2,19). Paul's weaknesses, on the other hand, prove that he is a servant of Christ (11:23). When he boasts about them (11:30), he does not boast as a fool, for he is speaking the truth. He refrains from boasting about his spirituality, however, "because I should not like anyone to form an estimate of me which goes beyond the evidence of his own eyes and ears" (v. 6; NEB).

To keep him from being too elated by "the extraordinary nature of these revelations" (JB), Paul was given "a thorn in the flesh, a messenger of Satan, to torment me" (v. 7; NIV). What Paul means by the thorn or stake in the flesh remains an enigma. While some have supposed it symbolizes a mental or moral problem, the thorn probably designates "a painful physical ailment" (TEV), though efforts to identify it as malaria, myopia, epilepsy, speech impediment, etc., represent sheer speculation (see Gal 4:13–15; 6:11; 1 Cor 15:8; 2 Cor 10:10). That the ailment seriously impeded Paul's work is indicated by its designation as an angel (or messenger) of Satan which harasses him (see 1 Thess 2:18).

In an effort to find a remedy for the malady, Paul three times "begged the Lord to rid me of it" (v. 8; NEB). Each time the answer came back, "My grace is sufficient for you, for my power is made perfect in weakness." Sermon possibilities abound in this text: on the answer to prayer (sometimes God responds in the negative); on the sufficiency of grace (God's grace makes it possible to endure pain, to rejoice in suffering; Rom 5:2–5); on power and weakness (God's power works in the weakness of the cross, which shows that love is the most powerful thing in the world; 1 Cor 1:25). Since the power of Christ is manifest in weakness, Paul will gladly magnify his weakness so as to be empowered with the might of God. Therefore, he can be content with "weakness, insults, hard-

ships, persecutions, and calamities" (v. 10). Crippled by the
thorn, and hindered by hardships, Paul attacks and over-
comes the principalities and powers (see Rom 8:38; Col 2:15).
He has learned an incredible truth: "When I am weak, then I
am strong."

Paul is now finished with boasting (v. 11). The Corinthians have forced him into this foolish self-defense. Instead of
receiving the false apostles (11:4, 13), the Corinthians should
have viewed the heretical invasion as an opportunity to commend Paul. He is not one whit inferior to these "super-
apostles" (NIV; see 11:5), even though he is nothing (10:10; 1
Cor 15:8–9; 1 Cor 4:13). Although the Corinthians seem blind
to the fact, "the signs of a true apostle were performed" before
their eyes. The Corinthians, with their penchant for showy
spirituality, supposed that the signs consisted of esoteric
practices like glossolalia and miracles (1 Cor 12:10). Paul, too,
could perform "signs and wonders and mighty works" (see
Rom 15:19). The difference is that Paul's signs were performed with "all patience" (Greek: "patient endurance"), that
is, performed in the midst of suffering; the signs of the cross
are the signs of authentic ministry. Yet, the petty Corinthians
still complain, disturbed by Paul's refusal to accept financial
support. Don't they understand that he declined for their benefit—to avoid being a burden? Paul throws up his hands in
sarcasm, "Forgive me this wrong!"

Apprehension and Admontion (12:14–13:10)

Paul is projecting a third visit to Corinth. The first was
his original mission (Acts 18:1–17), and the second, the
"painful visit" (2:1; see Intro.). When he comes, Paul "will
not be a burden" to the Corinthians (see 12:13). He will
maintain his practice of refusing monetary support (11:7–
10; see 1 Cor 9:12–18), "because what I want is not your
possessions but you" (v. 14; NIV). Paul's real concern is people (see 9:14; 1 Thess 2:19; 3:10), his purpose, the restoration
of harmonious relations with the Corinthians (see 2:3; 7:11).
There is a lesson here: the church is not primarily concerned
with statistics or budgets, but with persons—accepting
them and helping them to authentic self-acceptance. Paul
expands this point by drawing an analogy from the relation
of parents and children: "parents should make provision for

their children, not children for their parents" (v. 14; NEB). Paul, like a concerned parent (see 1 Cor 4:15), wants to supply the needs of the Corinthians (see Rom 1:11). He is willing, therefore, to "spend and be spent for their souls" (i.e. their lives). He "spends" by working to support his own mission (see 1 Thess 2:9), and he is expended by his suffering ministry which conveys life (4:12; see 1 Thess 2:8). This generous providing and spending may suggest that "I love you overmuch" (v. 15; NEB), but surely this does not mean that the Corinthians should love Paul the less.

The Corinthians' lack of love is confirmed by their accusations. While acknowledging that Paul has declined their offer of support, some of the Corinthians charge that Paul is a "crafty fellow" who trapped them "by trickery" (v. 16; NIV). Perhaps, they perceive Paul's refusal to accept their gifts as a cover for a larger deception—a ministry which is not authentically apostolic (see 12:11–12). At the same time, the Corinthians may be charging that Paul, while refusing support for himself, has taken advantage of them through those he has sent. Titus and the brother who accompanied him could have claimed the right to financial support from the churches (1 Cor 9:1–14). In no case, however, "did Titus defraud" (v. 18; NEB) the Corinthians. Titus conducts his activity in the same spirit of integrity that characterizes the work of Paul; they "take the very same steps" (Goodspeed). To follow "in the footsteps of Paul" should not mean to conduct a Mediterranean tour, but to become an imitator of him as he was of Christ (1 Cor 11:1).

At v. 19, Paul asks, "Have you been thinking all along that we have been defending ourselves to you?" (NIV). What else has Paul been doing for the last three chapters? However, the question is not *what* he has been doing, but before *whom*. Paul has not been "addressing our defense to you"; he has been "speaking in God's sight" (v. 19; NEB) in the presence of Christ (see 2:17). In the conduct of his ministry, Paul has to answer to God (Rom 14:10; 1 Cor 3:13), not to the Corinthians (1 Cor 4:3–4). Nevertheless, addressing them as "beloved," he is concerned about the edification of the church (10:8; 13:10), and he is apprehensive about his visit. He fears that when he comes he "may not find you as I want you to be, and you may not find me as you want me to be" (v. 20; NIV). In the latter case, the Corinthians might find that Paul has come "with a rod" (1 Cor 4:21; see 2 Cor 10:11; 13:2,10).

What Paul does not want to find in them is "quarreling, jealousy, anger," etc. (v. 20; see Gal 5:20)—the sort of disruptive evils which result from a rival mission (see 11:4,13,20). Paul is also afraid that he might be humbled again as he had been on the second visit (2:1, 5–6; 7:12). Though the Corinthians would be the immediate cause of his humbling, the ultimate source is God, the final judge of his mission's adequacy (v. 19). Paul would be humbled, indeed, if the Corinthians would still have failed to repent of their earlier sins—"impurity, immorality and sensuality" (v. 21; NASB)—sins which marked their life in paganism (see 1 Cor 6:9). Sins of this sort indicate that evils which disrupt the community (v. 20) also corrupt character (v. 21)—an appropriate homiletical theme.

Paul's projected third visit will take on a quasi-legal aspect. According to Deut 19:15, "Any charge must be sustained by the evidence of two or three witnesses" (13:1). Paul's use of this text probably indicates that he plans to deal with the facts as they really are. Possibly he views his third visit as a sort of third witness. On his second visit, he had warned the evil doers, and now he is warning them by letter. "When I come this time, I will show no leniency" (v. 2; NEB). For their part, the Corinthians suppose that Paul is the one who is on trial, and they seek proof that Christ is speaking through him (see 5:20). Paul, upon arrival, will give them compelling evidence: the potency of his chastisement of the unrepentant. Powerful action of this sort is modeled after Christ; "he was crucified in weakness, but lives by the power of God" (v. 4). This does not mean that the crucifixion represents weakness and the resurrection power; the cross is the supreme expression of God's power (1 Cor 1:24), and the resurrection shows that what appears to be weakness (the crucifixion) is in truth the power of God (see Rom 1:4). Similarly, the apparent weakness of Paul—his unimposing presence (10:10) and his suffering service (6:4–10; 11:23–29)—is in fact the sign that God's power is at work in his ministry (12:10). Since Paul shares the suffering of Christ (Phil 3:10; Gal 2:20), he is "weak in him" (v. 4); since he shares the power of Christ's resurrection (Phil 3:10), he will exercise the power of Christ in dealing with the Corinthians.

In the intense light of the cross, the Corinthians ought to examine themselves (v. 5; see 1 Cor 11:28). They have been putting Paul to the test when they ought to be testing themselves. The crucial question is, Are you "in the faith"; is Jesus Christ "in you"? (NASB). Faith is the original response to the Christian message (Rom 1:16; 3:22), and the believer continues to stand in faith (1:24; 1 Cor 16:13) and to "walk by faith" (5:7). This life of faith is characterized as life in Christ or Christ in you—a life conditioned by the presence of the redemptive power of God (see Rom 8:9–11; Gal 2:20). Though the Corinthians may fail the test, they ought to be able to recognize that Paul has passed; the credentials of his service (11:23–29) are the suffering marks of Christ (Gal 6:17). However, Paul's primary concern is that the Corinthians "may not do wrong" (v. 7); he prays that "all may be put right with you" (v. 9; NEB). As for himself, Paul is confident (see 1 Cor 4:3–4). He can do nothing "against the truth, but only for the truth" (v. 8). His ministry is characterized "by the open statement of truth" (4:2). Yet, for all the severity of his warning, Paul is hopeful that he will not have to be severe when he comes. He wiil surely use the authority which the Lord has given, but that authority is primarily constructive, given "for building up and not for tearing down" (v. 10; see 10:8). There is much for the preacher to learn from Paul in this passage: conducting a ministry which is "for the truth," exercising authority which is "for building up."

Exhortation, Greetings, Benediction

(2 Corinthians 13:11 – 14)

As in his other letters, Paul concludes this epistle according to the literary conventions of his day. Paul says, "Finally, brethren, farewell" (NASB: "rejoice"; NIV: "good-by"). They are encouraged to heed Paul's admonitions and to restore a harmonious relation in the church (see 12:20). If they do, the "God of love (used nowhere else in Paul) and "peace" (Rom 15:33; 16:20; Phil 4:9) will be with them. The Corinthians are called upon to "greet one another with a holy kiss"—a practice borrowed from the synagogue and becoming part of the worship of the Pauline churches (Rom 16:16; 1 Cor 16:20; 1 Thess 5:26). This probably indicates that Paul expects the letter to be read before the Christian assembly. He also sends along the greeting of "all the saints" (see 1:2), that is, the Christians in the place from which he writes, probably Ephesus (see 1 Cor 16:19). The threefold benediction is not found in the other Pauline letters; Paul prefers the simple expression, "The grace of our Lord Jesus Christ be with you" (1 Thess 5:28; 1 Cor 16:23). This may suggest that the trinitarian formula is a later liturgical addition. In any case, it summarizes Christian existence. Christians have been transformed by the grace of Christ (8:9); they have experienced the depth of God's suffering love (Rom 5:8); they continue to share the fellowship of life in the spirit (Rom 8:9).

Bibliography

Very good introductory articles on the city of Corinth and 1 and 2 Cor are found in *The Interpreter's Dictionary of the Bible* (Nashville: Abingdon, 1962) 1, 682–98; these have been updated in the Supplementary Vol (1976) 179–86. Extensive investigation of the background of the Corinthian correspondence is presented by John C. Hurd, *The Origin of 1 Corinthians* (New York: Seabury, 1965), and Walter Schmithals, *Gnosticism in Corinth* (Nashville: Abingdon, 1971), though many of their conclusions are questionable. A popular treatment of the relevance of 1 Cor for today's church is found in William Baird, *The Corinthian Church—A Biblical Approach to Urban Culture* (Nashville: Abingdon, 1964).

Among the more detailed commentaries are the first-rate works by Hans Conzelmann, *A Commentary on the First Epistle to the Corinthians* (Hermeneia; Philadelphia: Fortress, 1975); C. K. Barrett, *A Commentary on the First Epistle to the Corinthians* (Harper NT Commentaries; New York: Harper and Row, 1968), and the same author's *A Commentary on the Second Epistle to the Corinthians* (1973). Briefer, but still concerned with exegetical details, are Jean Héring, *The First Epistle of Saint Paul to the Corinthians* (London: Epworth, 1962), and the same author's *The Second Epistle of Saint Paul to the Corinthians* (1967). More popular and based on the NEB is the readable and reliable commentary by Margaret E. Thrall, *I and II Corinthians* (Cambridge Bible Commentary; Cambridge: University, 1965).

An excellent short introduction to the life, letters and thought of Paul is presented by Leander E. Keck, *Paul—and His Letters* (Proclamation Commentaries; Philadelphia: Fortress, 1979). A more extensive and highly regarded work is Gunther Bornkamm, *Paul* (New York: Harper and Row, 1969). Vol 1, of Rudolf Bultmann, *Theology of the New Testament* (New York: Scribner's, 1951) is probably the most important

investigation of Pauline thought to have been made in this
century. Useful for understanding issues raised in the Corinthians letters is Victor E. Furnish, *Theology and Ethics in Paul*
(Nashville: Abingdon, 1968). A collection of important essays
on Paul is found in Wayne E. Meeks (ed), *The Writings of St.
Paul* (Norton Critical Edition; New York: Norton, 1972).